The Lighthouses of Maine

Southern Maine and Casco Bay

The Lighthouses of Maine

Southern Maine and Casco Bay

Jeremy D'Entremont

To the Ramseys with all best wishes,

[signature]

3/30/16

Commonwealth Editions
Carlisle, Massachusetts

ISBN 978-1-938700-10-1

Published by Commonwealth Editions,
an imprint of Applewood Books
Carlisle, Massachusetts 01741
www.commonwealtheditions.com

Commonwealth Editions publishes books about the history, traditions, and beauty of places in New England and throughout America for adults and children.

To request a free copy of our current print catalog
featuring our best-selling books, write to:
Applewood Books
P.O. Box 27
Carlisle, MA 01741

Cover and interior design by Stephen Bridges

MANUFACTURED IN THE UNITED STATES OF AMERICA

The photo on the front cover is Whaleback Light.
The photo on the title page is Halfway Rock Light.

Contents

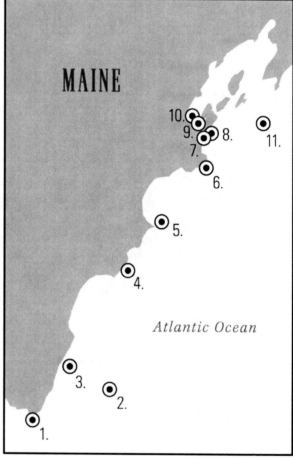

1. Whaleback Light
2. Boon Island Light
3. Cape Neddick Light
4. Goat Island Light
5. Wood Island Light
6. Cape Elizabeth Light

7. Portland Head Light
8. Ram Island Ledge Light
9. Spring Point Ledge Light
10. Portland Breakwater Light
11. Halfway Rock Light

Preface

From Kittery to Calais, the craggy, pine-lined coast of Maine is peppered with a spectacularly varied collection of lighthouses. Several are major tourist attractions, though many are offshore and out of sight of the average traveler. All of them have their compelling stories to tell.

Several of the state's most attractive and historic lighthouses are on the southern coast. Portland Head Light in Cape Elizabeth is the granddaddy of all Maine lighthouses, and its combination of history and scenic beauty is tough to match. The others in this part of the coast all have their own personalities: the postcard prettiness of Cape Neddick (the "Nubble"), the stark isolation of Boon Island, the rugged stone bulwarks of Whaleback and Halfway Rock.

In these pages, I've endeavored to go beyond these obvious descriptions to paint pictures of life at these outposts. With the automation of Goat Island Light in 1990, two centuries of lighthouse keepers in Maine came to a close. People still live at some of these lighthouses, but the traditional life of keepers is gone.

The more remote locations are uninhabited. One look at wave-swept Whaleback Lighthouse in a winter storm, with waves breaking over its lantern, and you can't help being profoundly amazed that people once lived within its granite walls.

In many cases, keepers performed extraordinary acts of heroism, saving lives in storms and shipwrecks. At some of the relatively comfortable stations on the mainland and sheltered islands, the keepers' heroism was generally of a quieter kind—the daily devotion to "keeping a good light" and fog signal.

This type of heroism, which played a significant role in keeping our nation's commerce moving safely, was generally underappreciated. It was the keepers and their families who brought these places to life. As much as possible, I've tried to use quotes from the keepers and family members themselves.

Now, in the age of automation, it's the preservationists who are, in many cases, bringing our lighthouses back from the dead. Their stories and struggles are included here as well.

I'll attempt to give thanks here to all those who have contributed in some way to this volume. As this book is the result of more than 25 years of research, I'm afraid I'll inadvertently miss someone. For that I sincerely apologize.

There have been many former light keepers, and family members of keepers, who have generously shared their stories. Not all are acknowledged in this preface, but their names appear throughout this book and I'm tremendously grateful to all of them. The men and women of the U.S. Coast Guard have always been there to help with research and transportation. I offer my sincerest gratitude to the staff of the Coast Guard Historian's Office in Washington, D.C.

The National Archives and its regional branch in Waltham, Massachusetts, have been treasure troves of vital historical materials. My special thanks go to Joan Gearin, who's been a great help at the Waltham facility.

Thanks also to the staff of the Library of Congress. Bob Trapani, Ann Trapani, and everyone associated with the American Lighthouse Foundation have provided invaluable assistance, as always. Bob is one of the leading champions of lighthouse preservation in the United States, and I can't thank him enough for his continued friendship and support.

I'm indebted to the staff and volunteers of the Maine Lighthouse Museum. I must mention the man who was responsible for the development of the museum, the late "Mr. Lighthouse," Ken Black. His friendship and knowledge are missed.

I offer a thankful nod to the staff of the General Services Administration in Boston, especially Saundra Robbins, Meta Cushing, and Sara Massarello. They've played an important role in lighthouse preservation in recent years, and I've greatly enjoyed visits to several lighthouses with them.

The Portsmouth (New Hampshire) Public Library and the Portsmouth Athenaeum were important in my research on the lighthouses of southern Maine. I particularly want to thank Jane Molloy Porter, the former keeper of the Athenaeum. Her comprehensive book, *Friendly Edifices*, is a wonderful resource as well as an inspiration, and she kindly shared her voluminous research material on Whaleback, Cape Neddick, and Boon Island.

The Rice Public Library and the Kittery Marine and Historical Museum have also been important sources for the lighthouses in that area.

Thanks also to the Town of York, the Friends of Nubble Light, the Old York Historical Society, and the York Public Library for information on Cape Neddick Light and Boon Island.

Chuck Petlick graciously shared material on his keeper ancestors, Leander and Arnold White.

Scott Dombrowski of the Kennebunkport Conservation Trust has always been generous with his time and boat rides to Goat Island. The Friends of Wood Island Lighthouse, especially Sheri Poftak and Brad Coupe, have been equally helpful.

The staff and volunteers of the Museum at Portland Head, particularly Director Jeanne Gross, have always provided kind assistance.

The Spring Point Ledge Light Trust and the Portland Harbor Museum helped with information on Spring Point Ledge Light and other lighthouses in the vicinity. The South Portland Historical Society provided valuable information on Portland Breakwater Light and other materials; special thanks to Kathryn Onos DiPhilippo, director of the society.

The Portland Public Library was another important resource. Thanks also to Jack Roberts of the City of South Portland for help with Portland Breakwater Light, and to Les McNelly for two memorable trips to Halfway Rock.

William O. Thompson, one of New England's great storytellers and the author of a number of volumes on lighthouse legends and lore, has always eagerly lent his knowledge and personal support, and I'm grateful.

Others whose friendship and support I want to acknowledge include Dolly Bicknell, James W. Claflin, J. Candace Clifford, Michel Forand, Brian Tague, Ross Tracy, Russ Rowlett, Marsha Levy, William Marshall, Seamond Ponsart Roberts, Elinor De Wire, and Vincent Salvatore.

My wife, Charlotte Raczkowski, is the most supportive lighthouse widow on the planet; I'm a very lucky man.

The late Connie Small, author of the book *The Lighthouse Keeper's Wife*, lived at several Maine light stations between 1920 and 1946. Her storytelling and her bright spirit were a joy, and she is sorely missed since her passing in 2005 at the age of 103. This book is dedicated to her memory.

CHAPTER 1

Whaleback Light in September 2007,
Photo by the author.

Whaleback Light

(Whaleback Ledge Light, Whalesback Light)
1830, 1872

Whaleback marks the approach to the harbor of Portsmouth, New Hampshire, and has often been referred to as a New Hampshire lighthouse, but this rugged granite tower is clearly in Maine waters by a few hundred feet. The jagged ledge known as Whaleback lurks menacingly on the northeast side of the entrance to the Piscataqua River, approximately a half mile south of Gerrish Island, part of the town of Kittery. The ledge, which is completely underwater at high tide, is, in fact, a continuation of the southern point of Gerrish Island.

Portsmouth, on the Piscataqua River, was established as an important port for shipbuilding and trade before the American Revolution, and the first federal shipyard in the United States was established on the Kittery side of the river in 1800. Wrecks occurred around the mouth of the river with sickening regularity.

One of the earliest known shipwrecks at Whaleback Ledge occurred in February 1733, when a schooner ran onto the rocks and suffered damage that eventually sank the vessel. Two of the five men on board drowned; the *Boston Newsletter* reported that the other three, "tho' much chilled with the Cold," were likely to survive.

In April 1821, the schooner *President*, heading to Thomaston, Maine, from Boston, struck the ledge. The vessel and its cargo were a complete loss. As the crew and passengers struggled in the waves, several boats full of soldiers arrived from Fort Constitution in New Castle, New Hampshire. Most of the would-be rescuers opted not to get too close to the ledges in the heavy seas. According to a newspaper account, Corporal George McAuley asked his crew, "Shall we save them or perish in the attempt?" The response was unanimously "Yes," and seven people from the wrecked vessel were soon rescued from certain death.

More wrecks followed in the ensuing years, including that of the Maine schooner *Fame* in October 1827. Congress had appropriated a sum of $1,500 in March 1827 for a lighthouse on the ledge, but that was plainly not enough money to build a lighthouse in such an exposed position. In February 1828, the sloop *Aurora Bartlett* from Newburyport ran into Whaleback Ledge, and the *Portsmouth Journal* asked, "How many more wrecks must be made before Congress will make an appropriation for this object [a lighthouse]?"

Two more appropriations were made by 1829, largely through the efforts of New Hampshire Representative Ichabod Bartlett. The three appropriations totaled $20,000. The first Whaleback (called "Whales Back" or "Whalesback" in early records) Lighthouse was constructed in 1829–30.

Daniel Haselton and William Palmer were the contractors who carried out the work. Haselton was a New Hampshire native who had built the Baptist church on Middle Street in Portsmouth. He later built the original stone lighthouse at Robbins Reef in New York Harbor (1839).

Nearby Wood Island was utilized as a base for the construction project. Work on the lower courses could take place only for a few hours around low tide. The lighthouse was erected on a conical granite pier, 42 feet in diameter at the bottom and 32 feet at the top. The 38-foot tower was 22 feet in diameter at its base, and 11 feet at the top.

To differentiate it from other aids to navigation in the vicinity, the lighthouse exhibited two fixed white lights, one 10 feet above the other. The lower light remained in operation until 1855. The upper light, in an octagonal wrought-iron lantern, was 58 feet above mean high water. Inside the tower were four rooms of living space on two levels, with a cellar. A wooden storage shed stood near the lighthouse. The first keeper, at $500 yearly, was Samuel E. Hascall, and the lighthouse went into service on September 16, 1830.

It was painfully clear that the tower had been poorly built; it leaked badly in storms and heavy seas. Winslow Lewis, a contractor who built many lighthouses, and Calvin Knowlton, a mason, surveyed the site and pointed out that the ledge hadn't been leveled before construction began, and that small stones were improperly used to fill in gaps near the bottom. They recommended that a breakwater be added on the eastern side of the tower, at a cost of $20,000. "This rock is favorable for erecting a breakwater in it," they concluded, "in the most permanent manner, and, if so built, would entirely protect the foundation of the light-house from any exposure from the effects of the sea, and remain for ages to come."

Some wooden sheathing added around the tower in 1837 apparently helped the problem of leaks, but Hascall reported that the tower rocked and shook increasingly in storms. Funds for the recommended breakwater were appropriated in 1837–38.

Lewis and Knowlton had devised no specific plan for the breakwater, so the local customs collector and lighthouse superintendent,

The first (1830) Whaleback Lighthouse. *U.S. Coast Guard.*

Daniel P. Drowne, brought in the famed Boston architect and engineer Alexander Parris as a consultant. Parris wrote that the lighthouse had been "constructed without science or workmanship." In one great storm on July 7, 1837, according to Parris, the vibrations were so violent that "some of the small stones of the tower were shaken out and fell upon the floors of the rooms, and articles of furniture were displaced by the motion of the tower."

Parris felt that a breakwater would afford little protection and advised instead that a new lighthouse be built for $75,000. He recommended a substantial masonry tower similar to the early wave-swept lighthouses in the British Isles. The great military architect Colonel Sylvanus Thayer concurred, saying, "It is expedient to take down the present structure, and erect in its place a good and substantial building." The breakwater was never built, and nothing would be done for more than 30 years other than repairs to the existing structures.

A storm in January 1839 dislodged a giant rock that tore away the iron ladder on the foundation. The assistant keepers, working in the lantern room, couldn't hear each other speak during the gale because the shaking of the apparatus was so violent.

A newspaper article said that the "stout heart" of Joseph L. Locke of Rye, New Hampshire, the principal keeper in 1839, "quailed when he heard the waves dashing furiously around his isolated tenement, the mad ocean forbidding his departure and threatening every moment to engulf the whole concern."

That might help explain why Locke, who had formerly been the keeper of White Island Light, New Hampshire, hired someone to do the work for him and spent little time himself at the lighthouse. He was dismissed in early 1840, in spite of his protests that he had been ill. Three more principal keepers came and quickly went in the next two years.

Lighthouse keeper appointments were highly political during this era. In May 1841, when John Kennard of South Berwick, Maine, a Democrat, was removed in favor of the Federalist Joseph B. Currier, surprise was expressed in the *New Hampshire Gazette:*

> Here is a young man who has been doing a good business in town at butchering . . . withdrawing himself from the pleasures of society, to be immured in a narrow dark, stone cell, rising from a sunken rock in the midst of the sea—a building accessible only in mild weather, and in storms is lashed from its base to its summit by the angry sea, which shakes it even to its foundation. And all this he is to endure and perform the duties of the station, too, for the sum of $600 per annum. Really, we should think a birth [sic] in the State Prison, aside from the disgrace attached to it, would be quite as agreeable.
>
> Yet notwithstanding the isolated situation of this light, there have been numerous applicants for it, not only now but in times past. It is not so much to be wondered at in an "old salt," who has been accustomed to a similar mode of life in his "wooden walls," but for a landsman, like the new incumbent, to desire the berth, evinces either a remarkable taste, or a remarkable love of office.

The *Portsmouth Journal* reported that a September 1841 storm caused the building to "rock like a cradle," and that the keeper "expected every moment that it would be carried away." The "landsman" Joseph Currier resigned a short time later, after just a few months as keeper.

Stephen Pleasonton—the Treasury official in charge of the nation's lighthouses—was a notorious penny pincher, but he agreed with the conclusions of Parris and Thayer. In 1838, he suggested a granite tower similar to one then under construction at Saddleback Ledge, at a cost of $15,000. Congress made no appropriation, and Pleasonton wrote the following in 1842:

> The light-house, though the plan was an excellent one, and if carried fully into effect would have endured for ages, was in one respect

infamously built, and that was fatal to the whole structure. The contract provided that the rock on which it was built should be reduced to a perfect level, and that all the bottom stones, to be of the large size, should be bolted to it; instead of which, the then superintendent, whom I shall not name, suffered the contractors to lay the stone upon the uneven surface of the rock, and fill up the crevices with small stones, easily washed out; and the water, once getting access, progressed to undermine the work in such a manner that I expected it would have fallen two or three years ago. . . . I am in daily expectation of information that the present building has been demolished by the force of the sea.

In his landmark 1843 report to Congress, the civil engineer I. W. P. Lewis (nephew of Winslow Lewis) was blunt, as usual, in his criticisms:

This pier is laid up dry, without bed or build to the courses, without any attempt to level the uneven surface of the ledge on which it rests. . . . On the pier thus rudely and fraudulently constructed, was erected a stone tower thirty-two feet high . . . and this was cased on the sea-side with wood, but only "for the comfort and health of the keeper, at the inconsiderable expense of $307.38." Here is a contract specimen, costing upwards of $20,000, constructed of solid masonry, or intended to be, and yet so fraudulently done (although supervised by some very honorable person, whose name is suppressed from motives of delicacy) that the miserable expedient of a wooden jacket over a stone tower is required, to make the keeper healthy and comfortable. Every subsequent year, up to the time of this inspection, repairs have been continually required, and workmen were employed at the time of my visit in securing the foundations with heavy iron bands and straps. No human art can, however, make a firm structure of it.

Lewis noted that the stones in the tower were laid without mortar or cement. A few iron dowels held the stones together "at rare intervals." He expected that the tower would be "demolished in some severe storm, if not taken down and rebuilt in a proper manner." Eliphalet Grover, previously at Boon Island, was the keeper at the time of Lewis's report.

A letter from Alexander Parris was included in Lewis's report. "Light-houses are a kind of building that should last for ages," he wrote, "and be constructed of the best materials and workmanship that can be procured, which is not likely to be had under contracts made at the lowest rate of prices." The overriding concern of saving money at all costs would finally become a thing of the past with the formation of a new federal lighthouse board in 1852.

The iron bands put around the foundation as reinforcement—added at the suggestion of the local lighthouse superintendent—soon broke away in winter storms. A sum of $25,000 was appropriated for the building of a new tower in 1847, but the old one was refurbished instead.

Jedediah Rand of nearby Rye, New Hampshire, was principal keeper from 1849 to 1853. The lighthouse later became a "stag" station with male keepers only, but the families of some of the early keepers lived in the tower. Rand generally had one of his children with him. In September 1849, his 15-year-old daughter, Elizabeth Jane, spent three weeks at the lighthouse with her father.

On September 25, Rand launched the station's small boat to take his daughter to New Castle, but it was swiftly overturned by a large wave. The keeper swam to his daughter and pulled her to his side as he clung to the bottom of the boat. Another wave righted the boat and threw the pair into the ocean; again Rand pulled his daughter to safety. A third wave upset the boat. By this time, Elizabeth had lost all her strength. Her father held her tightly and hung onto the boat. Elizabeth muttered, "Father, do I not love you . . . I want to go to heaven," just before she lost consciousness.

The crew of a passing schooner heard Rand's cries for help. A boat was dispatched to rescue the Rands, and they were taken to New Castle. Before they reached land, the apparently lifeless Elizabeth was revived. It was reported that her strong attachment to her father led her to return to the lighthouse with him that same afternoon, rather than recover with strangers in New Castle.

An 1850 inspection report mentioned that some repointing was done around the base and that the lantern and dome had been painted inside and out. A report of the colonel of the Corps of Topographical Engineers in the same year stated that the lighthouse, being essentially a harbor light, was not worthy of the expenditure necessary for a granite tower. "A light, however," the report stated, "upon a suitable iron framing, would cost much less and would answer all purposes." The report suggested that an iron pile tower could be built for $31,000, requiring only $6,000 more than had already been appropriated in 1847. The proposed tower was to be similar to the one then under construction at Minot's Ledge, south of Boston Harbor. The Minot's Ledge tower fell into the sea during a storm in April 1851, taking the lives of two keepers. That tragedy may have convinced the authorities that such a tower would have been ill advised at Whaleback Ledge.

A fourth-order Fresnel lens, displaying a fixed white light varied by more intense flashes every 90 seconds, replaced the earlier lighting apparatus in 1855. A new revolving fourth-order lens was installed in 1898.

In the early hours of February 15, 1863, the British schooner *Rouser*, on its way to Boston from St. John, New Brunswick, was wrecked close to Whaleback Ledge. It was reported that the lighthouse keeper, Joel P. Reynolds, looked out the window of the tower at 5:00 a.m. and saw a piece of the wreck, along with three men. One of the men called to the keeper, pleading for him to throw them a line. The keeper immediately complied, but the seas were too rough for the men to be saved. All seven men on board the *Rouser* died in the tragedy.

Soon after the wreck, a new fog bell and tower were installed at the lighthouse. The bell tower, which went into service on August 1, 1863, was described as a "frame structure, 25 feet high, whitewashed, standing upon the Light House pier, and attached to the southerly part of the Light House tower." When needed, the bell was struck by machinery every 15 seconds.

Gilbert D. Amee went to Whaleback as an assistant keeper in August 1864, and he soon succeeded Ambrose Card as principal keeper. In November 1864, Amee's wife, Mary (Baston), was officially appointed an assistant—the only woman keeper in Whaleback's history. Mary Amee developed tuberculosis and died onshore at the age of 32 in December 1867.

A sensational story emerged a few months after Mary Amee's death. Gilbert Amee continued living at the lighthouse with his 14-year-old daughter, Lucy, and his 5-year-old son. Isaac W. Chauncey was hired as an assistant on January 1, 1868. Less than three months later, at the end of March, there was a newspaper story proclaiming a "beastly outrage" at Whaleback, and shocking allegations of rape against Chauncey.

Amee said that he had a dream one night that his dead wife was calling to him. He awoke to hear his daughter's "stifled shrieks" and rushed upstairs to her room. He claimed that he found Chauncey, who was about 55 years old, in bed with his daughter, "she screaming and fighting him." After confronting Chauncey, Amee rang the fog bell for assistance. Help didn't arrive until morning, and in the meantime, Amee claimed, Chauncey threatened him with a hatchet. Amee armed himself with a knife and a gun in self-defense.

A doctor's examination revealed that Lucy Amee showed some "slight evidence that she had been unfairly and harshly dealt with," but there were no marks of violence on her body. The outcome of the case isn't clear, but it never went to trial. Chauncey had many friends in the community who believed him innocent, and the charges were apparently dropped.

In spite of the light and fog bell, the area was still treacherous in bad weather. In February 1871, a Nova Scotian schooner ran onto the ledge in a blinding snowstorm. The vessel broke apart and the crew was lost. While walking the shore, William C. Williams of Kittery, later a keeper at Boon Island, found letters and books that had belonged to the crewmen. Williams wrote that he "thought of the dear friends that would see them no more."

Ferdinand Barr, a Civil War veteran, was the first assistant keeper beginning in 1868, and he advanced to principal keeper in March 1871. Just three months later, Barr drowned in heavy seas while away from the lighthouse tending his lobster traps. According to a newspaper report, "a signal of distress was made from the light-house by his children, who were alone at the time, the mother being in this city, and though the watchman at the U.S. Hospital on Wood Island, Mr. James Andrews, and a fisherman named Wallace, went to the rescue, it was too late, as the unfortunate man had disappeared." Barr was said to be a Prussian by birth. He was about 30 years old and left his wife and three children.

Storms in 1869 had caused cracks in the lighthouse tower and its base, and a report stated, "The station should be rebuilt as soon as possible." Congress appropriated $70,000 for this purpose in July 1870. The Lighthouse Board called the location "one of the most difficult to work upon on the coast, as the rock is covered by the waves except at low water and is exposed to the full force of the Atlantic."

The new tower, 27 feet in diameter at its base and 50 feet tall to the lantern deck, was constructed of granite blocks dovetailed together in similar fashion to Minot's Ledge Light in Massachusetts and England's Eddystone Light. General James Chatham Duane, engineer for the Lighthouse Board's first and second districts, was involved with the design. The granite came from the Goodwin Granite Quarry in Biddeford, Maine, and was supplied by the partnership of Gooch and Haines.

The work of leveling the ledge began in the summer of 1870. The original tower remained standing while the new one was built. The process was slow, as it could take place only at low tide. The 1871 annual report of the Lighthouse Board announced that the masonry had been completed to a height of 20 feet above the low water mark.

The laying of the last stone in August 1871 was followed by the installation of the lantern and other ironwork and the lighting appara-

Early-1900s postcard view of Whaleback Light and the adjacent fog signal tower. *From the collection of the author.*

tus. The tower is lined with brick and has hard pine floors, cast-iron staircases, and iron ceilings. Horizontal I-beams lend support for each of the four floors. A basement provided storage space for water and fuel.

William H. Caswell was the principal keeper when the new tower was being completed, and his son, Frank, was one of his assistants. In November 1871, Caswell proclaimed the new tower "perfectly safe" and noted that it didn't even tremble in a storm. By the 1872 annual report, the new tower had gone into operation. At the time it was built, the focal plane height was reported as 68 feet, but the height is given as 59 feet on recent light lists.

Complaints that the fog bell couldn't be heard in thick weather led the *Portsmouth Journal* to proclaim, in early 1877, "The interest of commerce and the claims of humanity require some immediate action in regard to a steam whistle at Whale's Back." Action was swiftly taken, and beginning later in 1877, the old lighthouse tower served as a fog signal house upon the installation of a new Daboll fog trumpet.

Access to the rickety old tower was difficult in rough weather, however, so a new plan was devised. In the summer of 1878, a new cast-iron tower was built just to the north of the 1872 lighthouse to serve as a fog signal house. The tower, about half as tall as the lighthouse, was surmounted by a long iron pipe and a third-class fog trumpet that emitted an eight-second blast every 30 seconds. The original lighthouse was torn down by June 1880.

The fog signal tower was painted red for some years, and painting it was a precarious proposition for the keepers. In late June 1882, assistant keeper John Lewis fell from the tower as he was painting the apex of the pipe that held the foghorn. A tugboat transported him to shore, but he died from his injuries several days later at his home in Kittery.

A storm in February 1880 displaced one end of the bridge leading to the fog signal tower and caused an iron hoop used to reinforce the old lighthouse base to come loose. The hoop, according to a newspaper account, "flopped about in lively style with anything but musical noise."

A winter gale in 1886 sent waves smashing through a window of the tower, flooding the living quarters. Leander White, the principal keeper since 1878, displayed a blanket from the tower as a distress signal. Days passed before the seas were calm enough for two Kittery residents, Walter S. Amee and Samuel Blake, to reach Whaleback to rescue the occupants. The party's small boat then had trouble reaching Portsmouth Harbor, as the seas were still high. They were towed to safety by a steamer.

Leander White, seen here with his wife, Elizabeth, was the principal keeper of Whaleback Light 1878–87. His career also included 21 years at Maine's Cape Elizabeth Light. *Courtesy of Chuck Petlick.*

At first, the surviving base from the original tower served to protect the funnel-like opening between the lighthouse and fog signal tower. The base was in rough condition by the time of a newspaper article in August 1886, which stated that many of the large stones had been torn away by the action of the sea. What was left of the base was for the most part destroyed in a March 1888 storm.

A new 20-foot-high protective bulkhead,

built of pine timbers and planking, was bolted to both towers and to the ledge itself. The space between the bulkhead and the towers was filled with masonry from the old base. Another storm in November 1888 demolished more of the remnants of the original lighthouse's base and swept away a derrick being used for the bulkhead project. The storm left as much as 2,000 tons of granite from the old base piled against the lighthouse, which made access difficult. It was believed that the timely erection of the bulkhead had saved the station from even greater damage.

The storm also cut away the gravel from one side of the fog signal tower below its iron plates and washed away some of the concrete from its lower section. The scattered masonry from the old base was shifted and packed to provide a surface for a new boat slip, and the exposed lower part of the fog signal tower was covered by an apron of heavy stones from the old base, set in concrete and secured to the ledge. After some additional repairs, the station was pronounced "in excellent condition." Another storm in 1892 left huge stones blocking the entrance to the lighthouse.

Daniel Stevens of New Castle became an assistant keeper in 1887. Stevens would later become the highly respected keeper of the light-house at Monhegan, but he ran into some trouble during his stay at Whaleback. In May 1888, it was reported that he had gone ashore to get medicine for his wife, who was ill. While in Portsmouth, Stevens became intoxicated and was seen by several witnesses in front of a saloon plunging a knife into the chest of a local man, Bernard Johnson.

Stevens had to be overpowered by police and was locked in a cell. Johnson's injury proved not to be serious, and when questioned a few days later, Stevens said he remembered nothing of the incident. The outcome of the case isn't clear, but Stevens soon resumed his duties and remained at Whaleback until 1890.

Walter S. Amee of Kittery, the nephew of Gilbert Amee, became principal keeper in 1893. Amee had gone to sea as a young man aboard the Kittery-based schooner *Eldorado*. He stayed ashore when the vessel left for a fishing expedition on the Grand Banks in 1873. That proved to have been a wise decision, as the vessel and its crew were never heard from again. Amee went on to captain fishing schooners out of Salem, Massachusetts, and Portsmouth, New Hampshire, before brief stints as an assistant keeper at Boon Island, Maine, and White Island, New Hampshire.

Amee remained in charge until 1921, a remarkably long stay at a difficult offshore station. His first assistant keeper for most of those years was John Wetzel of Portsmouth, who held the position from 1897 to 1924. John Brooks of Kittery was the second assistant keeper from 1899 to 1915. The three men obviously had to have a congenial relationship in the confined quarters, and a 1911 article in the *Boston Globe* stated that they refused offers of positions at other Maine stations. At the time of that article, the men each spent four days on duty followed by two days onshore. That schedule was often disrupted by rough weather and sea conditions. It was said that up to that time, Amee had spent only 11 days out of sight of the lighthouse in 18 years.

Amee performed a brave rescue during a storm in August 1899, when a small boat with two men aboard capsized near the lighthouse. While one of the assistant keepers blasted the foghorn repeatedly in an attempt to get the attention of the men at a nearby lifesaving station, Amee launched the small lighthouse boat and managed to haul the drowning men aboard.

In July 1911, two young men from York, Maine, were entering the Piscataqua River in their powerboat when it hit a rock and developed a fast leak. Their cries for help were heard by Amee, who launched a boat and reached the men, then took them back to the lighthouse for the night.

John Wetzel died suddenly at his home in Portsmouth in December 1924. Wetzel, who had tended the range lights at Henderson Point in Kittery before taking the first assistant position at Whaleback, was only 57 years old; his death was attributed to a cerebral hemorrhage. The *Portsmouth Herald* described him as a "man of quiet tastes and generous disposition."

Arnold White was keeper at Whaleback Light 1921–41. *Courtesy of Chuck Petlick.*

Arnold B. White of New Castle, New Hampshire, son of the former keeper Leander White, succeeded Amee as principal keeper in 1921. He would be the station's last civilian keeper.

When the Coast Guard took over operation of the nation's lighthouses in 1939, keepers were given the option of joining the Coast Guard or serving out the remainder of their careers as civilians. White joined the Coast Guard in 1941, shortly before he was transferred from Whaleback to Portsmouth Harbor Light, New Hampshire. Maynard Farnsworth, an assistant under White since the 1920s, became the next Coast Guard officer in charge in 1941.

Arnold White was in charge when Justine Flint of the *Portsmouth Herald* described a visit to Whaleback Ledge in 1939:

> *On arriving at the landing-stage of the light, Captain Arnold B. White, the keeper, was waiting with a smiling welcome. . . . Captain White has lived in this solitary wind-swept setting for 18 years and once during that time when ice filled the Piscataqua in 1924 he was unable to go ashore for 14 days. Because the government rules that only members of the crew may live there permanently, his wife must remain in town. Visitors are welcome, however, and Mrs. White often spends several days with him.*

The assistants at the time were Maynard Farnsworth and Warren Alley. Flint described the cellar as "scrupulously clean." A walled-in window was used as a cupboard for food supplies. A cistern in the cellar held drinking water, brought from Sebago Lake 2,000 gallons at a time. The next level contained a small kitchen, "comfortable and cheerful, with good sized windows to admit air and sunshine." The writer was amazed that the men were excellent housekeepers; the numerous brass articles were "kept as bright and glowing as a mirror."

Testifying to the men's exemplary work, the government awarded an efficiency pennant to the crew in 1938. The award was given for an inspection rating of 95 percent or better. White explained his general philosophy: "The government tolerates no excuses. You must anticipate trouble and have spare parts on hand at all times."

Maynard Farnsworth, seen here with two unidentified women, was one of the keepers at Whaleback Light from the 1920s into the 1940s. *Courtesy of Chuck Petlick.*

Flint noted that the tower's 10 windows—the glass a half-inch thick—were screened to keep out the houseflies that sometimes arrived in swarms. When asked what the men ate, White explained that they had once tried a system whereby one man was cook for the day. That didn't last, because their tastes were all different.

Lobster was a staple, and peaches and cream was a preferred dessert. White's dumplings were "an epicurean's dream." This praise has been echoed by White's daughter, Marion White Petlick of Rye, New Hampshire, who fondly recalled visits to the lighthouse as a girl in a 2004 interview. Her father usually had some kind of baked treat, such as bread pudding, cooling on a windowsill.

The principal keeper's quarters were on the floor above the kitchen, and everything was neat and orderly, the furnishings modest. A barometer hung on the wall; the keepers were required to fill out weather reports every four hours. A ship's medicine chest was also kept in this area. White told of a visitor who had once slipped and cut her arm on the rocks. He dressed and bandaged the woman's injury, and a doctor later said that he had done the job perfectly.

A new, more powerful foghorn was installed in the fall of 1939. Portsmouth police said they were inundated with calls from residents who were startled by the strange, loud "groaning noise." A short time later, the station was converted to electric operation.

In December 1948, the historian Edward Rowe Snow, famed as the "Flying Santa" to lighthouse keepers, dropped a bundle from a plane containing Christmas gifts for the keepers at Whaleback. Snow's first drop was too far away for the keepers to recover. Three weeks later, a man walking on a beach in Sandwich on Cape Cod found the package, 90 miles from where it had been dropped. Years later, the man still had the book that was in the package, Snow's *Storms and Shipwrecks of New England*.

A 1957 story in *New Hampshire Profiles* magazine reported that the Coast Guard keepers had two days' leave between eight-day stays at the lighthouse. There were quarters for four in the tower, but there were usually two or three on duty at one time. The young keepers frequently had to work on the compressors in the fog signal tower, where temperatures could reach 145 degrees and the noise was deafening. The article described the difficulties the Coast Guardsmen sometimes had getting on and off the station. Engineman Third Class Francis D. Hickey left to go ashore on New Year's Eve in 1956, only to lose his power. His boat drifted for six hours before the crew of a Coast Guard cutter located him.

A storm in February 1960 did severe damage to the boat slip and caused considerable shifting of the station's protective riprap stone.

The light was automated in mid-January 1963, and the Fresnel lens was replaced by rotating aerobeacons. The change rendered the light brighter; it went from 50,000 to 3.5 million candlepower. An emergency generator was installed as a backup to a cable from shore. The cast-iron fog signal tower was torn down after automation.

In 1991, the Coast Guard found that the fog signal was causing structural damage to the tower, so they lowered its volume. In the fall of 2002 the rotating aerobeacons were replaced by a smaller VRB-25 optic. More recently, a VLB-44 solar-powered LED optic has been installed.

In 2009, under the provisions of the National Historic Lighthouse Preservation Act of 2000, ownership of the lighthouse was transferred to the American Lighthouse Foundation (ALF) and its local chapter, the Friends of Portsmouth Harbor Lighthouses (FPHL).

There are plans to install a dock to facilitate restoration and visitation. There is much deterioration inside the tower, and costs are expected to run into the hundreds of thousands of dollars. It will be a challenge, but ALF and FPHL plan to restore the lighthouse and to eventually open it for limited public tours. You can learn more at www.portsmouthharborlighthouse.org.

Whaleback Light can be seen from Fort Foster in Kittery; Fort Constitution, Fort Stark, and Great Island Common in New Castle, NH; Odiorne Point in Rye, NH; and other spots on both the New Hampshire and Maine sides of the Piscataqua River.

Sightseeing boats from Portsmouth pass close by, including many of the cruises offered by the Isles of Shoals Steamship Company. Phone (800) 441-4620 or 603-431-5500 or visit www.islesofshoals.com. The daily sailings of Portsmouth Harbor Cruises also provide a view; (800) 776-0915 or 603-436-8084; www.portsmouthharbor.com.

CHAPTER 2

Boon Island Light in August 2008. *Photo by the author.*

Boon Island Light

1811, 1831, 1855

In the summer of 1682, a coastal trading vessel, the *Increase*, was wrecked on an unnamed island about 400 square yards in size, only 14 feet above sea level at its highest point, several miles off the towns of York and Kittery in southern Maine. The four survivors spent a month on the island, living on fish and gulls' eggs. One day they saw smoke rising from Mount Agamenticus several miles away, so they built a fire in response. The Indians at Mount Agamenticus saw the smoke from the island, and the stranded men were soon rescued.

The most famous incident in the island's history was the wreck of the British ship *Nottingham Galley* on December 11, 1710. Some survivors struggled to stay alive for more than three weeks, finally resorting to cannibalism. Kenneth Roberts fictionalized this harrowing story in his 1956 novel, *Boon Island*.

It's been stated that the men from the *Increase*, seeing their survival as a boon granted by God, were moved to name the island Boon. In fact, the island was referred to by that name long before 1682. John Winthrop mentioned it in his *Journal* in 1630. It seems more likely that the island's name stemmed from the practice of local fishermen, who left barrels of provisions on the island for the benefit of shipwrecked sailors. That would certainly have been a "boon" in such circumstances.

In 1797, Benjamin Lincoln, local lighthouse superintendent, met with the Boston Marine Society to discuss the building of an unlighted beacon on Boon Island for the safety of local fishermen and coastal traders. An octagonal wooden tower was completed in the summer of 1799.

The tower survived until October 1804, when it was destroyed by a tremendous storm. A stone day beacon was erected in the summer of 1805. Three of the workers involved in erecting the tower drowned when their boat capsized as they left the island; only the boat's captain survived the incident.

A pair of shipwrecks in 1810 finally convinced the authorities that a proper lighthouse was called for. Lincoln recommended a lighthouse, and Albert Gallatin, secretary of the Treasury and in charge of lighthouses at that time, agreed. A sum of $3,000 was appropriated for the establishment of the light station, and two contractors, Noah Porter and Thomas Heath, completed the job for $2,527. The lighthouse, in service by the winter of 1811, exhibited a fixed white light 32 feet above mean high water. An octagonal iron lantern topped the 25-foot-tall tower, and its multiple lamps were hung on chains.

A letter from Albert Gallatin dated November 25, 1811, indicates that Benjamin Ware (or Wane) was appointed as the first keeper at a salary of $300 yearly. If he ever assumed his duties on Boon Island, Ware didn't remain there long. According to the historian Edward Rowe Snow, the first keeper—unnamed by Snow—resigned on December 16 after witnessing great billowing waves that swept over the island.

David Oliver, who had helped to build the station, was appointed keeper by the end of the year. It's not clear if Oliver ever actually took up residence on the island, either. On December 31, he wrote to the local superintendent: "I have made a calculation and find that what would make me comfortable would amount to nearly five hundred dollars—also the wages of a Man and Boy would be thirty dollars a month. Therefore on these considerations I feel myself inadequate to the task, unless government will supply me with some of the above stated articles."

The government was unwilling to match Oliver's demands, and he soon left to serve as the mate on a Europe-bound ship. Thomas Hanna, a sea captain originally from Scotland and the grandfather of the Cape Elizabeth Lighthouse hero Marcus Hanna, was appointed as keeper in March 1812. A letter from Isaac Ilsley, the customs collector at Portland, described him as an "active capable man."

Hanna accepted the position for a yearly salary of $300 and an advance of $100 for provisions. He moved to the island with his wife and two sons, aged 12 and 14. The pay was clearly inadequate, consid-ering the extremely harsh conditions. Hanna wrote to Henry A. S. Dearborn, the customs collector in Boston, in March 1813: "It will be one year on the first of April next since I have lived on this desolate island and discharged my duty faithfully in taking care of the Light-House. . . . I now must state that unless the Government provide for me and my family as agreed, I shall on the first day of April leave this place. If the sum of $150 be added to the salary ($300) I shall be satis-fied and will provide for myself."

Hanna was soon granted a pay raise of $100 yearly. He resigned three years later, in May 1816. Hanna expressed a desire to get his old job back in 1818, and he later became the keeper at Franklin Island

Light. The next keeper at Boon Island, the former mariner Eliphalet Grover—a York, Maine, native born in 1778—served a remarkable 23 years at the station.

In April 1817, the *Portsmouth Oracle* reported that Grover had been awakened at about 2:00 a.m. by the barking of his dog during a storm. Upon hearing "the crying of persons on the island," Grover dressed and went outside. At the south side of the island, Grover discovered a small vessel and its crew struggling to break free of the rocks. The keeper summoned his two sons to help. They swiftly launched a boat, and as they neared the other vessel the last words heard from it were, "Come out quick with your boat." The vessel disappeared, and no sign of it could be found in the morning. Grover believed that it had gone to the bottom.

In the winter of 1821, Grover passed the time by fashioning a fiddle from pieces of red spruce and pine roof shingles. In his 1894 history of York, George A. Emery wrote that Grover presented the fiddle to York's First Congregational Church in 1834. John S. Thompson, who later became keeper at Boon Island, "extracted its dulcet and harmonious strains for the benefit of that congregation," according to Emery.

The "Boon Island fiddle" has survived for almost two centuries and is now in the collection of the Old York Historical Society. Steven Mallory, a musician and historic preservation expert, has written that Grover's workmanship reflected "someone who was definitely an experienced, talented, and versatile joiner and carver, but who had little time or opportunity, and no necessity, to learn the finer points of violin making." Mallory has restored the fiddle and used it to record a CD of old tunes.

Grover's log also resides at the Old York Historical Society. Here are some excerpts, preserving Grover's spelling:

> March 6, 1829: *The Sea racked my slip all to pieces. The lower part gone and middle part the bolts broken of and the upper part rotten and tumbled down so that it all wants to be made new.*
>
> October 31, 1829: *At 9 PM all my famely was forst to go to the Lighthouse and Stay until 5 next morning. At our return to the house found all our water gone and all the platforms gone and all my turnips and cabage washt away and my walls all Down. I have been hear 13 years 4 months 28 days and never see such a time before. The sea washd the small rocks from under the Lighthouse and Dwelling house the island was all under water for 4 hours.*
>
> July 1, 1830: *My Boat got very much injured by beeing driven against thee rocks so that she cant bee repaird.*

January 1831: *16 day and night the island all under water the most part of the time and the Sea and Large Rocks that washt up against the Slip has rackd it to the westward Some parts of it 2 feet. From the 15 until the 17 as Dismel a time as I ever had sence I have Been on Boon island.*

The roof of the lantern was replaced after the 1829 storm. By early 1831, the lighthouse was in such poor condition that it needed to be replaced. Congress appropriated $4,000 for a new tower in March 1831, and the contractor hired to build the lighthouse was Seward Merrill of Gorham, Maine.

The first stone for the tower was laid on May 31, 1831. In an 1842 letter to Nathan Cummings, superintendent of Maine lighthouses, Grover wrote that the mortar used by the masons in the rubblestone tower "did not suit" him because "there was too much sand in it." He continued: "I made them put in more lime. From that time, until the light-house was done, the mortar was made well; all was made with fresh water and fresh sand, and I did my utmost to have it done well."

The new lighthouse went into operation on July 21. It stood 49 feet tall, with an octagonal wrought-iron lantern. The light was 69 feet above mean high water, its 12 lamps backed by 14-inch reflectors. After the new lighthouse was completed, Grover was ordered to take the 1811 tower down to a height of 12 feet to be used for wood storage.

Lighthouse keeping positions were political appointments at this time, and it was unusual for someone to serve an uninterrupted stint at a single station as long as Grover's. Attempts to wrest Grover from the position started as early as 1818, when a "layzy idle fellow" spread a rumor in the Portsmouth press that he had died. Grover responded in a letter to the local lighthouse superintendent: "I hope that the government is not going to remove me to gratify one man unless I have done something worthy of being removed. There is many people that would like well to have my pay but few would like the birth [*sic*]."

In 1837, a letter written by a local resident, Samuel Cushman, called the keeper "a profane man, uncivil to those who visit the island" and charged that he had been living "in great intimacy" with his wife's sister. (Grover apparently was separated from his wife, who was ill.) Another local man accused Grover of assailing a government agent who was attempting to retrieve a buoy that had drifted to the island, "with a volley of vulgarity and abusive oaths seldom equaled any where else."

At a hearing in April 1838, Grover was absolved of charges of misconduct and destroying a buoy, but he had enemies in the community and his days on the island were numbered.

Newspapers published Grover's account of a storm in January 1839. The seas broke over the island, forcing Grover's family to take refuge in the tower. The ocean broke into the front of the dwelling and "unhung the doors," as seawater filled the lower rooms. Water also entered the lighthouse tower, leaving shells and seaweed everywhere. An 80-foot covered walkway between the house and tower was swept away. As the storm died down, the family "beheld an astonishing spectacle." Fragments of wood were scattered over the island, and boulders were torn from their former resting places. The high seas continued for three days after the storm.

Life on Boon Island was harsh, but Grover's saddest log entry came after he got word that he was being replaced:

> May 10, 1839: *Turnd of [sic] of Boon Island after Serving as Lighthouse Keeper 22 years and 10 months and 20 Day Without Cause.*

The poet and author Celia Thaxter described Boon Island Lighthouse in her 1873 book, *Among the Isles of Shoals,* as "the forlornest place that can be imagined." She related the memories of a man who had grown up on the island—possibly Eliphalet Grover's son, Samuel Grover. The man "described his loneliness as something absolutely fearful, and declared it had pursued him all through his life. . . . He spoke with bitterness of his life in that terrible solitude."

Mark Dennet (sometimes spelled Dennett) of Kittery, Maine, followed Grover as keeper. John Thompson, a shipmaster, succeeded Dennet in 1841. After a storm in October of that year, Thompson told his son in a letter that the gale had changed the face of the island so much that "an old acquaintance would scarcely believe himself on Boon Island." He continued:

> *The storm commenced on the night of the 3d and continued with unabated fury 30 hours, wind veering and hauling from NE to ESE. The tides being very full, the whole island was underwater about three hours each high water—and the sea making an uninterrupted breach over the whole island, overturning huge rocks which had probably rested in quiet for centuries, to find a new resting place. Among others, a huge rock, which has been located (since time began) about half way between the highest part of the island and low water mark, now rests on the highest part of the island; the weight of this rock I will not attempt to conjecture. . . . It will remain a monument of the resistless power which placed it where it is now.*

The storm knocked away the northeastern part of the dwelling, undermined the front porch and ripped up the floor, moved two 400-gallon cisterns, and drove the boathouse from its position. Four barrels of oil were upset and 168 gallons were lost.

When the civil engineer I. W. P. Lewis visited the island for his landmark 1843 report to Congress, he found much to criticize: "Tower of rubble masonry . . . laid up in bad lime mortar, which has given way to the effects of moisture and frost; base rests upon the uneven surface of a rock . . . tower leaks in all directions; staircase rotten and unsafe to use; window frames and casings also rotten and leaky; walls inside covered with ice in winter and green mould in summer; whole structure in bad condition."

The keeper's tiny dwelling, consisting of two rooms downstairs and two attic chambers, was just as poorly built and leaky as the 1831 tower, according to Lewis. He emphasized the light's importance, pointing out that it was "extremely valuable, not only as a coast light and point of departure for Portsmouth harbor or Cape Elizabeth lights, but as a mark to clear the very dangerous ledges lying between it and the main land." Keeper Thompson, wrote Lewis, was often away and hired a man to keep the light in his absence. The keeper had been off the island for a week at the time of Lewis's visit.

John Kennard of South Berwick, Maine, who had lost his keeper position a few miles down the coast at Whaleback Light for political reasons, became keeper in 1843. Thompson complained in a letter to President John Tyler: "I have been a seaman from a boy—being now 60 years old, am poor, have a family to support, with little or no means. I voted for your excellency for Vice president and intended to exert my feeble influence to promote another election for you for President— why I am removed, I am at a loss to determine."

A few months later, Kennard was charged with negligence by a local captain, who said he wasn't able to see the light at a distance of four miles on a certain night. An investigation showed that snow had obscured the light on the night in question, and Kennard was exonerated. Just the same, he lost his job for being a Democrat in 1846, when the political winds again changed. Capt. Nathaniel Baker of York was appointed to succeed him.

The schooner *Caroline* was wrecked on the island in 1846, and Baker rescued the crew. Nevertheless, three years later a petition circulated for Baker's removal. An assistant keeper, Benjamin O. Fletcher, wrote to the secretary of the Treasury in Baker's defense, calling him "a man of strict integrity of character" who had always "kept a good light."

In spite of this recommendation and others, Baker was dismissed a short time later. John Thompson, who apparently had made friends in high places since his earlier dismissal, succeeded him. The local lighthouse superintendent, Augustus Jenkins, complained, "no man could do more to keep a better Light than Capt. Baker."

An article in the *Portsmouth Journal* described a summer visit by schooner to Boon Island from York in 1849, while Thompson was keeper.

> *Here are we met by Captain Thompson, who receives us cordially. . . . Capt. T. then leads us up the immense steps, laid by nature, to his dwelling, pointing us, on our way, to a rock, weighing many tons, which the ocean in a violent storm rent from its bed and tossed far up on the island. While Mr. Fletcher prepared the "chowder," Capt. T. shows us over his farm of ten square feet of land, and his inexhaustible quarry of granite. . . .*
>
> *As we go to other portions of the island, large flocks of sea-birds alight almost at our feet, and our murderous propensities long for a gun; but though Capt. T. has a fine double-barrel fowling piece, he will not let us disturb his little visitors, as they fly to his hospitable island.*

In November 1849, Thompson wrote a letter to the local superintendent describing the vessels he had counted passing the island in the preceding month: the total was 1,050, and 935 of them were schooners. Thompson made a case for an upgrade in the power of the light, concluding, "I doubt if there is any Light on the United States Atlantic Coast more needed than Boon Island Light."

An 1850 inspection report noted that the lighthouse was leaky and that a new tower and dwelling were much needed. The old system of 12 oil lamps and corresponding reflectors was still in use at the time.

The present lighthouse was constructed in 1854, along with a new dwelling, after an 1852 appropriation of $25,000. The first stones were laid in June, and the tower was completed by September. A reporter for the *Portland Argus* wrote that 1,800 tons of granite from a Biddeford, Maine, quarry were used in the tower, and it was lined with 70,000 bricks.

Ira Winn fabricated the bronze lantern and the tower's iron stairs in a Portland machine shop. Winn later wrote: "When this light was completed the members of the Light House Board of Washington visited it. They were so pleased with the work they ordered one of the same size made of iron to go to California." Winn is also credited with the construction of lanterns at Portland Head, Cape Elizabeth, Wood

Island, Seguin, Halfway Rock, Pond Island, and Whaleback, among others. He built the stairs inside many Maine lighthouses as well.

George Bowden of York was keeper during the rebuilding. An assistant was assigned to the station at this time, at a yearly salary of $300. The principal keeper's yearly salary in 1854 was $600.

At 133 feet tall (118 feet to the base of the lantern), the extant tower is the tallest lighthouse in New England. It's 25 feet in diameter at its base and 12 feet in diameter at the top. An additional $19,973 was appropriated in 1854 for "procuring illuminating apparatus, and completing the light-house tower and buildings." The powerful new second-order Fresnel lens, made by Sautter et Compagnie of Paris, went into operation on January 1, 1855.

Joseph H. Hart, principal keeper beginning in 1859, reported to the Lighthouse Board the number of vessels seen passing near the island during the year 1860: 13,653, or more than 37 per day on average. Of those, 12,680 were schooners.

Edwin J. Hobbs of Hampton, New Hampshire, who had circumnavigated the globe as a mariner, came to Boon Island as an assistant keeper in 1874. In 1876, his 14-year-old daughter, Annie Bell (or Annabelle) Hobbs, wrote an essay about life at Boon Island for a children's magazine called *The Nursery:*

> *Out at sea, on a rock eight miles from the nearest point of land and about nine miles east of the town of Kittery, is Boon Island, upon which I have been a prisoner, with the privilege of the yard, the past two years.*
>
> *I will give you a description of the place and its inhabitants. The island is made up of nothing but rocks, without one foot of ground for trees, shrubs, or grass. Now and then sails dot the wide expanse, reminding me that there is a world besides the one I dwell in, all surrounded by water.*
>
> *The inhabitants of this island consist of eight persons just the number that entered the ark at the time of the flood. There are three men, the three keepers of the light, whose duties are to watch the light all night, to warn the sailors of danger. There are two families of us, and in my father's family are five members. There are but three children in all, —my little brother, Stephen Green, three years old, little Mamie White of the other family, a little girl of four years; and myself, Annie Bell Hobbs.*
>
> *Our colony is so small, and the children so few, that the inhabitants have concluded not to build a schoolhouse. Consequently I have my father and mother for teachers. The whole number of*

scholars in my school last year was two: my little brother and myself. The books used were "The Nursery" and "Emerson's Arithmetic."

After school hours, I turn my eyes and thoughts toward the mainland and think how I should like to be there, and enjoy some of those delightful sleigh rides which I am deprived of while I am shut out here from the world. In the summer we have quite a number of visitors, who board at the beaches during the season. They come to see the lighthouse and all it contains; and we are very glad to show them all, though it is quite tiresome to go up into the light a number of times during the day, since it is one hundred and twenty-three feet from the rock on which it stands to the light.

Up there among the clouds, my father and the other keepers have to watch, night after night, through storms as well as pleasant weather, through summer and winter, the year round, from sunset to sunrise; so that the poor sailors may be warned off from danger.

Edwin Hobbs went on to serve as principal keeper at White Island Lighthouse, New Hampshire, from 1876 to 1880.

Alfred J. Leavitt of Hampton, New Hampshire, was the principal keeper from 1874 to 1886, after five years at White Island. In May 1885, the *Portsmouth Journal* reported that Leavitt's rowboat, loaded with coal and groceries, had capsized on the Piscataqua River while the keeper was on his way back to the island from Portsmouth. Leavitt managed to cling to the overturned boat until it sank, and he struggled

Boon Island circa 1880s. *From the collection of the author.*

to stay afloat until a rescue boat arrived. According to the newspaper, after Leavitt's boat sank and discharged its cargo, it surfaced again "with the snort of a puffing pig."

The slender lighthouse tower sometimes swayed and vibrated in high winds, and water frequently entered the tower during storms. This was solved by the addition of six sets of iron ties, with struts, attached to the top of the lantern and anchored to the masonry 40 feet below the watchroom gallery. The 1888 annual report of the Lighthouse Board added that new double windows were installed, the floor was raised by 18 inches, and the tower was thoroughly repointed.

The granite keeper's dwelling also had problems with leaks because of "defective linings and a defective roof," and it was cold and deemed unsuitable for occupation. The house was largely rebuilt, and a wood-frame second story was added in 1889. In the following year, a stone-and-brick oil house was built. The station's 1,200-pound fog bell was repositioned onto a belfry atop the oil house, to be rung by hand in response to signals from vessels. An additional wood-frame, one-and-one-half-story, six-room keeper's house was added in 1904, and it became the home of the principal keeper and his family.

Capt. William Converse Williams, a native of Kittery, went to Boon Island as second assistant keeper in 1885. He advanced to first assistant in late 1886, and then became principal keeper on November 21, 1888. He went on to serve 23 years in the position, earning $760 yearly without a single raise.

Keeper William C. Williams and his wife, Mary Abbie Williams. *Courtesy of the Old York Historical Society.*

Williams, who worked in construction as a young man, married Mary Abbie Seaward of Kittery, and they had three children: Charles, Lucia Mabel, and Bertie (who died in childhood). A 1926 newspaper article described Williams, who was known as "Willie": "He was a tall, spare, man, dignified, and a refined gentleman of the old school. He had a soft, low voice, and his language was marvelous for its simplicity and purity. He had an optimistic disposition, nothing ever worried him and he never got excited. He was neat and methodical even in performing the simplest task."

At the age of 90, Captain Williams recounted his experiences at Boon Island to Robert Thayer Sterling, author of *Lighthouses of the Maine Coast and the Men Who Keep Them*. Williams had many pleasant times at Boon Island, but he recalled the danger of the job:

> *There were days when I first went on the station that I could not get away from the idea that I was the same as locked up in a cell. . . . All we had was a little stone house and a rubblestone tower. When rough weather came we didn't know as it would make much difference as to whether we went into the tower or not, for a safe place. The seas would clean the ledge right off sometimes. It was a funny feeling to be on a place and know you couldn't get off if you wanted to, and tidal waves was all the talk in the early days. Take it with me, I was a young fellow and had never been placed in such a situation. When the terrible seas would make up and a storm was in the offing, I was always thinking over just what I would do in order to save my life, should the whole station be swept away.*

Williams described the experience of keeping watch in the tower during bad weather:

> *There was no lounging place at the top of the tower, only an old soap box or camp stool for a seat. As you set there just watching your light, all the enjoyment you got was hearing the wind making a cotton-mill din around the lantern. With such a noise and being so many feet up from the ground, the seas battering the rocks down below is utterly drowned out. . . . One can hardly believe that after a storm you would find the big plate glass windows of the lantern covered with salt spray, at that distance in the air. After some storms the spray on the glass would be so thick and dimmed with bird feathers it would require a whole day to clean things up before lighting-up time.*

In an 1888 storm, Williams and the others on the island had to take refuge at the top of the tower for three days. Compared to this storm, said the keeper, the famous Portland Gale of November 1898 was "just a breeze." In a January 1896 storm, Williams and his wife again took shelter in the tower as high seas completely surrounded the dwelling.

The *Portsmouth Herald* published vivid details of a gale that began on January 31, 1898. The temperature was two below zero, and thick ice formed on the lighthouse and other buildings. The ice was so thick that the fires in the stoves inside the dwellings had to be extinguished for a time because the chimneys were blocked. For nearly 24 hours the winds blew at 75 to 100 miles per hour. The seas moved two water tanks, each weighing approximately four tons, about 75 feet. "It was the hardest night we ever passed," said Williams, "and no one slept on the island the entire night." Williams called the unusual sight of the island completely encased in ice "one of the grandest sights" he had ever witnessed. The oil house belfry that held the fog bell was so clogged with ice that it took several hours of chopping with axes to get the bell working again.

A telephone system connected the watchroom in the tower with the bedrooms of the keepers in 1902, but contact with the mainland was more problematic. In the days before a telephone cable reached the island, carrier pigeons were sometimes used for emergency communications. One of the birds reportedly made the trip to the island from Portsmouth in 10 minutes.

In an attempt to brighten up the island in summer, Williams brought barrels and boxes of soil out from the mainland every spring so that the families could enjoy a small flower garden during the summer. With the next winter's gales, the soil would always be washed away. "I did not care so much about it myself, " Williams said later, "but it was hard for the children who passed the vacation months and were so interested in seeing flowers in bloom."

One Thanksgiving, Williams and his assistants were unable to go ashore to buy a turkey. Providence intervened on the night before the holiday when a dozen black ducks smashed into the tower, providing the keepers with their Thanksgiving dinner. This was not an unusual event; in December 1876 it was reported that 11 migrating geese flew blindly into the lantern and were killed. Even with a shorter tower at the time, the *Portsmouth Journal* reported in 1849 that it was not uncommon for "several bushels" of dead birds to be found around the tower in the morning.

A number of vessels were wrecked around Boon Island during Williams's stay. In August 1892, the fishing schooner *Alabama* was lost on a nearby ledge during a squall, but the crew made it to the island and spent the night at the keeper's house. About four months later, the 96-ton Nova Scotian schooner *Gold Hunter,* with a cargo of hardwood, was dashed on Boon Island Ledge, about three miles east of the island, when the temperature registered four below zero. Williams later described what happened next:

The crew succeeded in getting into their yawl boat and after a six hour row reached the light station at 1:30 in the morning. We were aroused by the barking of the dog. . . . We got our lanterns and climbed down over the icy rocks and made out the little boat just outside the breakers. The castaways were instructed to follow the lights around the rocks to the lee of the island, and then, still guided by the glimmer of the lanterns, watched their chance to run in on the top of a sea. The three keepers, covered with flying spray, grasped the boat rails and the dog at the same time took the painter [a rope attached to the bow] in his teeth and ran up the rocks. The little craft was hauled beyond the reach of the next sea.

The dog who took part in the rescue was Prince, described as a yellow Irish setter. The crew of six from the *Gold Hunter* included a cabin boy, only 14 years old. The keepers and their wives resuscitated the nearly frozen men, and after a few days at the station they were able to return to the mainland. Years later, Williams boarded a passing boat to put some mail on board, and he was happily greeted by Zippy, the cabin boy he had saved.

Getting on and off the island was hard enough in calm conditions, but frequently a risky proposition when the seas grew heavy. On one occasion in April 1890, Williams and his wife, with two workmen, set out for Portsmouth in a sailboat. The vessel was overturned by a sudden squall near Gerrish Island in Kittery. The four passengers managed to cling to the boat until a schooner from Rockland rescued them.

The keeper's son, Charles, served as second assistant briefly, then as first assistant from 1897 to 1905. Charles married Susannah Whittaker of Fall River, Massachusetts, in early 1898. They arrived at the island just as the great gale of January 31, 1898, was sweeping in. Charles and his wife lived on the island until their children were old enough for school; he vowed that his children would get the education he had missed.

During a shore visit in December 1900, Charles Williams described a storm that had swept the island a few days earlier. He had stood watch through the night in the tower, and he said that it seemed that the tower would topple over. The lighthouse shook, he said, with such violence that his teeth chattered involuntarily.

After his lighthouse days, Charles Williams served as an ensign in the U.S. Navy during World War I, worked at the Portsmouth Naval Shipyard, and served as a selectman in Kittery from 1937 to 1946. He was a deputy sheriff during Prohibition, when rumrunners were active in the area. On the occasion of his 100th birthday in 1974, the *Ports-*

Keeper William C. Williams (standing at far right) with family members on Boon Island around 1900. The keeper's son, Charles, is standing next to him, and his wife, Mary Abbie Williams, is seated, second from right. *Courtesy of William O. Thomson.*

mouth Herald called him "a strong man, creating an innate respect for the rightness of things."

Elaine Wood of Portsmouth interviewed Charles Williams in 1968, and the interview was included in William O. Thomson's book *Solitary Vigils at Boon Island*. The keepers' tasks were sometimes dangerous, as he explained: "The scariest job was the job of painting the black cap on the lantern. This has to be done once a year. A rope is thrown up around the ball and lightning rod, and tied on the gallery rail, so as to make a loop. When this job is done all other work on the island stops and all the islanders stand to watch the man who has volunteered to do the painting."

In 1910, one of William C. Williams's grandchildren, Mary Luther Lewis, wrote an article about life on Boon Island. The keepers took turns keeping watch, she recalled, with rotating shifts. As a girl, Mary loved to roller-skate on the island's boardwalks. Summer visitors from York were frequent, and her grandmother often made fish chowder for them. The family liked to sit on the rocks outside to eat their lunch, which typically consisted of lobsters and lemonade.

Mary Luther Lewis's daughter, Eunice Lewis Evans, later wrote down some of the stories passed to her by her mother. Chores assigned to the children included dusting and polishing the brass in the house, picking caterpillars from the flowers, and killing flies. (They were paid a penny per caterpillar or fly.) Keeper Williams had a lobster trap for each of his grandchildren, and the money made from the catch was added to their bank accounts. There would be an evening church service, and everyone was in bed by 8:00 p.m. to be ready to start the next day at 5:00 a.m.

Another assistant keeper under William C. Williams was Charles Allen, who went to Boon Island in 1907. Allen's wife, Minnie Scovill Allen, was the sister of Connie Small, author of the book *The Lighthouse Keeper's Wife*. Allen played the trumpet as a hobby, something not appreciated by the other keepers. To keep everyone happy, he agreed to play the instrument only when he was on solitary watch in the watch room, near the top of the tower.

Robert Thayer Sterling, who wrote about William C. Williams years after his retirement, observed, "To walk about his front yard without risk of being washed into the sea is a pleasure, and with that comes contentment." Williams, one of the best-known lighthouse keepers in Maine, died in 1939 at the age of 93.

Surprisingly, although it was considered an important seacoast light station, Boon Island for many years had only the hand-operated bell as a fog signal. In October 1897, Capt. R. D. Evans of the Lighthouse Board said that he had been unable to hear the bell when passing the island in the fog. The board recommended a more effective fog signal, at a cost of $10,000.

The request for an appropriation was repeated yearly from 1901 through 1909, but it wasn't granted. Apparently, it was believed by some that the whistling buoy placed some distance away at Boon Island Ledge in 1882 filled the role of a fog signal. A horn wasn't installed at the station until 1959.

Roger Paul Philbrick of York served as first assistant keeper from 1913 to 1918; Mitchell Blackwood was the principal keeper for part of that time. Philbrick's daughter, Eva, later recalled that "Boon Island Fish Chowder" was a major draw for tourists who visited the island from York. Fresh fish, mostly haddock donated by local fishermen, was the primary ingredient. The chowder was simmered in a big black pot over an open fire, stirred with long, oarlike paddles. Perhaps not coincidentally, Philbrick later became the proprietor of the Galley Restaurant at York Harbor.

Eva Philbrick wrote down some of her memories many years later. There were two other little girls on the island, the daughters of the other keepers. When the other girls were away, Eva had to play by herself.

I really had a wonderful imagination. I played on the big rocks, which were my ships, and all the seals lying in the sun were my army, and the big spouting whales passing by were my submarines.

In 1915, there was a truck driver from Boston who came out and covered himself with Vaseline, and swam from the island to my grandfather's wharf in York Harbor. That was nine miles.

You had to be very neat and you never knew when the inspectors were going to arrive, at least once a month or one in two months. They wore white gloves and would go over the top of the doors and windows, then look in every closet.

My mother was from Boston and she was only 23 years old when we went to live there. She never could get used to the sound of the ocean. Me, I love it.

Five navy men were sent to Boon Island to serve as lookouts during World War I. Minnie Smith, whose husband, Harry, was principal keeper from 1916 to 1920, cooked for the men along with her own considerable family of 10 children. Minnie, who was in the U.S. Naval Reserve, was possibly the only enlisted woman ever to live on the island. Her husband retired in 1945 after 35 years of living at lighthouses along the Maine coast.

For a time during the World War I era, there were so many children living on the island that the state provided a teacher. Lilla Severance Cole, who graduated from the Castine (Maine) Normal School in 1915, was the traveling teacher for the children at Boon Island and several other light stations for a few years. She later taught at the West School in Portland for more than 40 years. The duties of a teacher at island lighthouses were varied; they sometimes included helping with household chores or assisting the keeper's wife with dressmaking. The life was often exciting, too. Once, on the way to one of her island stops, Cole was thrown into the ocean when the boat overturned. She and her luggage were recovered safely.

Travel to and from Boon Island was always one of the banes of a keeper's existence. In March 1930, two assistant keepers were returning from Cape Neddick with a boatload of furniture when rough seas caused a line to become snagged in the boat's propeller. The vessel was disabled and the men drifted helplessly until a lifesaving crew from the Isles of Shoals arrived. The lifesavers tried to land the keepers at Boon Island but found it impossible, so the men spent the night at the Coast Guard station at the Isles of Shoals.

Another undated story concerns keepers who were marooned on the island for weeks by bad weather. Their food had almost run out when they sent a bottle adrift containing an urgent plea for help. A passing schooner picked up the bottle and managed to get a barrel of food to the keepers, which may have saved their lives.

A strange episode in August 1933 had a happy ending when newspapers reported that 50-year-old principal keeper Harold Hutchins, after being reported missing a few days earlier, was found in Ellsworth, Maine, which was his birthplace. He had left the island on a shopping expedition. The episode was attributed to mental problems brought on by sunstroke. Hutchins retired from the Lighthouse Service a short time later.

Hutchins's daughter Shirley Kelly was later interviewed. She went to Boon Island as an infant in 1924, when her father was transferred from White Island Light Station, New Hampshire. Shirley later lived at York Beach with her mother and siblings during the school year, but she looked forward to summers on the island.

> *There was always something to do on the island. We made kites and flew them anytime, as there was always a breeze coming off the ocean. On the Fourth of July we sat on the rocks and watched the fireworks from the mainland. . . . We sat there, drinking hot chocolate, and "oohed" and "ahhed" every time there was a burst of light on shore. One Fourth of July we had a hail storm and put out a big pail and got enough hail so Mom could make ice cream. What a treat!*

Harold Hutchins's wife, Addie S. Hutchins, composed a poem called "The Lighthouse Sunset, July 1930," reproduced in Thomson's *Solitary Vigils at Boon Island*. The last three verses summed up her philosophy, which was probably shared by many who have lived on the island:

> *Life's not all sunshine and roses*
> *We have our troubles to bear*
> *But if we have a smile for things worthwhile*
> *We'll find contentment there.*
>
> *I learned a little lesson*
> *As I stood by the lighthouse tall*
> *And gazed at the beautiful sunset*
> *The peacefulness over all.*
>
> *God's works are all so lovely*
> *Wherever one may be*
> *And I have found contentment*
> *On a lighthouse by the sea.*

The light was electrified in 1931, which increased the candle-power to 75,000 and made Boon Island the most powerful light between Cape Elizabeth and Graves Light in Boston Harbor.

Florence Idella Batty, the wife of Fred C. Batty, an assistant keeper, was interviewed when she was 90 years old. She recalled a particularly memorable storm on October 29, 1932:

> *We had this wicked storm and Fred's watch was from 6 when he lit the light till 12 o'clock at night and then he'd go call another keeper to relieve him. Well, I always set up to keep him awake. He'd read, I'd sew, I'd crochet and I crocheted a whole spread that winter.*
>
> *I was reading a book called* The Harvester *and was really interested in it and had it pretty near read and I said to Frederick at 12 o'clock I wanted to finish the book. About a half an hour afterwards, and my Lord, first thing I heard this terrible racket and Fred come running down the stairs and the sea had come up and had hit the front of the boathouse and the house and come right into my front hall and filled that front hall. . . . I said, "I'm not going to be surprised if a rock come in any time." I hadn't gotten that out of my mouth when in come this rock. Broke the door down, and he happened to have a board, a piece of plank and he got that into the house and braced the door back as best he could and we bailed water all the rest of the night. That was on the turn of the tide and that's what made that so terrible. You couldn't get off that island for a month, I swear. Nobody could get off it.*

Howard "Bob" Gray, the son of a longtime Maine light keeper, Joseph M. Gray, became an assistant keeper in 1932. Gray's son, Howard Jr., was born ashore in York during the October gale of that year. It was weeks before someone was able to reach the island with news of the baby's birth.

A contingent of Coast Guardsmen was stationed on the island during World War II to keep an eye out for German U-boats. One of the men, 22-year-old Calvin Dolby, lived on Boon Island with his 19-year-old wife, Miriam, and their baby daughter. Miriam (Dolby) Hammel later described the experience for *Lighthouse Digest*:

> *One day there was a terrible storm, so terrible that we went to the top of the lighthouse and sat with our heads almost in our laps so we wouldn't hear the storm. You can imagine my daughter between my legs, crying . . . the dog trying to climb onto me (she was so scared), me sitting on the floor by the light, my husband trying to calm me. . . .*

We had clotheslines strung up along our wooden walk and Cal would help me hang out the sheets. Sometimes, the wind was so strong it would rip the clothes off the lines . . . then we would have to go rescue them off the rocks. At times, whatever blew off blew into the ocean. I lost a couple of favorite blouses that way.

During the summer it was lovely. Never too hot, always a cool breeze. Lots of seals to watch, whales out in the ocean, dolphins to see once in a while, and the opportunity to go fishing whenever you wanted to.

We were even fortunate enough to witness the surrender of a German sub directly off Boon Island. We went to the top of the lighthouse and stepped outside and with binoculars watched the sub surface where our Coast Guard boat was waiting. Saw the hatch of the sub open up and the men come out. It gave us a feeling of pride and relief. I am so glad that I witnessed this event.

In his book *Storms and Shipwrecks of New England,* Edward Rowe Snow wrote of a powerful storm that hit the island in November 1945. John H. Morris was in charge at the time and was at the station along with his wife, Gertrude, their child, Lorne, and an assistant, Ted Guice. The storm was threatening to destroy the buildings, so Morris took his family to the second assistant keeper's house, which was partly sheltered by the tower, and they weathered the storm. All communication with the mainland was severed. A few days later, emergency food supplies were dropped on the island from a helicopter. Morris later told Snow: "What really scared us was the sound that the rocks made as they hit against each other. Not a stone on the island was left unturned. The generator failed when a giant sea broke right into the engine room, and we had to operate for the rest of the storm with kerosene lamps. The waves actually climbed halfway up the side of the lighthouse tower itself. I shall never forget that Gale of '45."

During a stretch of rough seas in February 1947, two Coast Guardsmen—18-year-old Clifford Gustavson and 30-year-old Robert Adams—were left without food for a few days before a supply boat was able to reach them. The men were in no immediate danger, but it was reported that, as they took in a few notches on their belts, they found themselves looking longingly at passing seagulls.

A letter from Robert Quintern, a Coast Guard keeper, was published in the *Maine Coast Fisherman* newspaper in September 1951. Quintern reported that the crew had been busy "carrying forth one of the Coast Guard's finest traditions, which is 'if you can't move it, paint it.'" The men had just gotten a new television and were looking forward to watching baseball games. Catching fish was no problem, since there were plenty of "cod, cunners, and mackerel and a few lobsters."

Kendrick Capon was one of the Coast Guard crewmen for a time in the 1950s. One of the first things that impressed him was the initials and symbols that had been carved into many of the island's rocks over many years.

Forty years later, Capon told a writer for the *York Weekly,* "The island isn't much bigger than my yard, and after a while, you'd sense where the other person was. You'd become accustomed to hearing the sounds." One day, after becoming aware that the other keeper was not in the house, Capon looked outside to see the man, a steeplejack's son, shimmying his way down the lightning rod that runs the length of the tower. When he got halfway down, the copper rod began to cut into the man's hands. By the time he reached the bottom his hands were cut to the bone. "He was in bad shape," remembered Capon.

Capon recalled being stuck on Boon Island for 83 days in one stretch, living on bologna, bread, and crackers. Despite the hardships, he remembered his lighthouse days fondly. "After about the second or third day, you feel completely relaxed," he said. "I've never felt that relaxed since. I've never been able to capture that."

When Capon was at Boon Island, the Coast Guardsmen would pass the time by telling stories. "We would sit and tell ghost stories to each other until late and then we'd strap on a gun to go out and check the motors," he recalled.

Ron Schultz, on the island crew for several months in 1959, later remembered it as "good duty" for the most part. Landing the small boat on the boat slip was the biggest challenge. Attempts to land in rough conditions often resulted in a saltwater bath, and Schultz said there were always biting fish nearby that apparently liked the taste of Coast Guard flesh. One morning, Schultz and his fellow crewman "Moon" Mullen both lost their wallets when swells pushed them against the jagged rocks and ripped their pants.

Charles Eaton was one of the Coast Guard crew from 1962 to 1965. "I liked it there," he told a reporter in 2003. "We worked 14 days on and then had seven days off. There were four of us stationed there, and usually, it was two men at a time at the light. We were close enough to see the shore, but too far away to do anything about it."

Tom Dunwoodie of New Jersey was also on the crew in the early 1960s. He later told *Lighthouse Digest:* "Boon Island was probably the most relaxing lighthouse anyone could be stationed at. The ocean breeze with waves breaking on the rocks, along with the noise of seagulls and seals, made this a perfect setting. The weather did get bad at times, but this was also enjoyable. You could watch the waves hit the rocks and spray in the air all day. This sounds good now, but it is being recalled 40 years after the fact."

August "Gus" Pfister, on the crew in 1967–68, also described life on Boon Island as very relaxed. "We could spend time doing a craft or reading," In a 2004 letter, he wrote about the difficulties of access:

> *The most common method of getting to Boon Island from the mainland was by the weekly supply boat from Portsmouth Harbor Station. Getting from this boat onto the island was by one of the light station's small boats. These double-ended rowing boats, equipped with extra wear boards on the underside, would be slid down the ways, meet with the supply boat to transfer supplies and personnel, and then landed back on the station, the most difficult part of the operation.*
>
> *The boathouse was located near the western end of the island, with the slipways going down in the northwest direction. This spot often saw the waves going across the end of the slip, caused by waves and swells that came washing around the island's western end. The trick in getting back onto the ways was to approach near the end, watch for a slight lull in the waves, then row madly onto the end, get hooked onto the winch, and ride up the ways. Most of the time, it was not too difficult. But there were occasions when it did not quite go as planned. The rower had to watch carefully for the wave next to the one he chose to ride in on, and if it looked to be more than he liked, he would pull back out.*

The Coast Guard keepers reported weather conditions every three hours to Portsmouth, New Hampshire. They also monitored the Cape Neddick "Nubble" Light. When the light at Cape Neddick couldn't be seen from Boon Island, it was time to turn on the fog signal. Pfister recalled the nuances of the sound:

> *I found no problem with the sound, and easily worked and slept when they [the fog signal and related equipment] were in operation. Some of the other people did have some problems, but could eventually settle and ignore the noise. And the nature of the echo could give some indication of foggy conditions. When the weather cleared, the echo was a sort of gentle decaying sound. On rare occasions, we got a soft echo off a fog bank. And when really souped-in, the horn blast ended in total silence, as the fog just absorbed the noise. This was almost eerie in the lack of any echo.*

According to Robert Ellis Cahill's book *Lighthouse Mysteries of the North Atlantic,* many people have reported a ghost on Boon Island. The ghost stories are often tied to an enduring Boon Island legend that concerns a keeper of the 19th century who arrived at the island with his new bride. After a few happy months the keeper fell ill and died during a gale. His wife realized the importance of keeping the light and, despite her grief, managed to climb the tower's 168 stairs and light the lamp for the duration of the storm, which lasted several days. Soon after the storm ended local mariners noticed the lack of a light at Boon Island. They landed to investigate and found the young woman wandering the rocks aimlessly, driven mad by grief and exhaustion. The young woman supposedly died a few weeks later, and some claim her spirit haunts the island.

The ghost is described as "a sad faced young woman shrouded in white." Keepers and fishermen have seen this phantom, wrote Cahill. Some say the woman in white is the ghost of the mistress of the captain of the *Nottingham Galley,* while others claim she is the young bride whose husband died on the island one winter.

Bob Roberts, a Coast Guard keeper in the early 1970s, later said that the other keepers asked him if he believed in ghosts when he first arrived on the island. Roberts laughed at the time, but strange events soon had him thinking differently. He later recalled that doors in the keepers' house seemingly opened and closed by themselves, and the fur on the back of Smoky, the station's dog, would stand on end as if he saw a mysterious "something." When he would go outside to turn on the fog signal, Roberts said he felt as if "someone was watching."

One day Roberts and his fellow crewman, Bob Edwards, were off the island fishing. The men drifted too far in their boat to make it back to the island in time to turn the light on before sunset. There wasn't a person on the island, but somehow the light was glowing brightly by the time they returned.

Another former Coast Guard keeper, Dave Wells, later said that one time the station's Labrador retriever chased "something from one end of the island to the other and back again." The Coast Guardsmen couldn't see what the dog was chasing. "We figured the island must be haunted, but nothing ever bothered us," said Wells.

A severe storm in February 1972 destroyed the boathouse and swept boulders, along with five feet of water, into the keeper's house. The Coast Guard crew had to use a jackhammer to remove the giant stones. The fast-moving storm, with its 65-miles-per-hour winds, also shut down the station's generators. A backup kerosene lamp, known as "Aladdin's lamp" to the crew, was put into service in the lighthouse.

Even that wasn't as bad as the great blizzard of 1978. The February 6–7 storm, one of the worst in New England history, flooded the keeper's house to a depth of five feet and scattered boulders around as though they were pebbles. The two Coast Guard crewmen on duty were forced to take refuge in the tower. The following day they were removed by helicopter. It was estimated that $100,000 worth of damage was done at Boon Island by the blizzard of '78.

The station was scheduled for automation in 1980, but the blizzard moved up the schedule. The light and fog signal were automated by the end of 1978. The badly damaged keeper's house was deliberately burned; today only a fragment of its outer walls remains standing. Recent storms have continued to take their toll. The October 1991 "perfect storm" damaged doors, electronics equipment, and generators, putting the light out of commission for a time.

In 1993, the second-order Fresnel lens was removed and replaced by a modern optic. The Fresnel lens remained in storage at the Coast Guard's Aids to Navigation Team's facility in South Portland until April 2000, when it was put on display at the Kittery Historical and Naval Museum.

In May 2000, the lighthouse was licensed by the Coast Guard to the nonprofit American Lighthouse Foundation. On April 1, 2003, the "Republic of Boon Island" declared its (fictional) independence in an effort to raise preservation funds by selling citizenships and political offices. In 2012, it was announced that the ownership of the lighthouse would be transferred to a new steward under the guidelines of the National Historic Lighthouse Preservation Act of 2000. At this writing in early 2013, that process is in progress. If no nonprofits or communities step forward to apply for ownership, the lighthouse will be auctioned to the general public.

Boon Island Light can be seen distantly from spots onshore, including Sohier Park in York, but it's best seen by boat. Friends of Portsmouth Harbor Lighthouses may offer views from occasional lighthouse cruises; visit www.portsmouthharborlighthouse.org for more information.

CHAPTER 3

Cape Neddick Light in August 2008. *Photo by the author.*

Cape Neddick Light

(Nubble Light)
1879

A short distance off the eastern point of Cape Neddick in the town of York, about two miles north of the entrance to the York River and a mile south of the entrance to the Cape Neddick River, is a high rocky island—about two and a half acres in area—known as the Nubble. It's separated from the area now known as Sohier Park on the mainland by a narrow channel, about 100 feet wide, that's almost dry at low tide. The explorer Bartholomew Gosnold, who met with local Indians there in May 1602, dubbed the island Savage Rock.

One of Gosnold's crew, John Brereton, wrote:

> *From the said rock came towards us a Biscay shallop with sail and oars, having eight persons in it, whom we supposed at first to be Christians distressed. But approaching us nearer we perceived them to be savages. These coming within call, hailed us, and we answered. . . . They spoke divers Christian words and seemed to understand much more than we, for want of language to comprehend. . . . These much desired our longer stay, but finding ourselves short of our purposed place, we set sail westward, leaving them and their coast.*

A member of Capt. John Smith's crew, circa 1614, has been given credit for naming the Nubble (often spelled "Knubble" in old records). This is the best known of several New England nubbles. The word *nubble* is defined as "a small knob or protuberance" by the *Random House Dictionary;* it's an old diminutive of *knob* or *nub.*

The geographic boundaries of Cape Neddick are somewhat confusing. Cape Neddick Village and the cape that terminates near the Nubble are separated by the resort area of York Beach, which was developed after the entire area was named Cape Neddick. The peninsula that terminates at the Nubble is also known to locals as "Cape Neck." The area was thriving with shipbuilding, fishing, and lumber exporting in the 19th century.

Many local mariners had requested the placement of a lighthouse on the Nubble as early as 1807. Congress appropriated $5,000 for this purpose in 1837, but Capt. Joseph Smith, who had traveled the coast extensively as the captain of a U.S. revenue cutter, recommended against a lighthouse at the Nubble on the grounds that enough lights were already in operation in the vicinity. Instead, he recommended an unlighted beacon at York Ledge, about two miles offshore from the Nubble, and a lighthouse at Stage Neck, at the entrance to the York River, which would render the river entrance "both easy and safe." An unlighted monument was erected a short time later at York Ledge, designed by the renowned architect Alexander Parris.

Even after the death of 15 people in the November 1842 wreck of the bark *Isidore,* north of the Nubble near Bald Head Cliff, it still took nearly four more decades before the lighthouse was established. The *Isidore,* according to legend, reappears now and then as a ghost ship with a phantom crew.

New calls for a lighthouse resulted in another congressional appropriation of $5,000 in 1851, but again the project died after some debate. The idea was revived again in 1874, when the Lighthouse Board requested $15,000 for a lighthouse "for the benefit of the coasting trade." The request was repeated in the following year, and Congress made the appropriation in July 1876.

There was a delay in procuring the site, which was the property of multiple owners. Because tourism in the area was on the rise, there were plans for a hotel on or near the island. The bargaining process moved the project back to early 1879, when the island was purchased for $1,500.

The station was constructed under the supervision of Gen. James Chatham Duane, an engineer with the Lighthouse Board. The iron sections were manufactured in Portland and then transported to the island aboard the U.S.S. *Myrtle* in April 1879, and the buildings were completed by June. At first the tower was painted reddish brown; it's been painted white since 1902.

The 41-foot cast-iron tower, lined with brick, was first illuminated on July 1, 1879, with a fixed red light exhibited 88 feet above mean high water from a fourth-order Fresnel lens. A 32-step cast-iron spiral stairway led to the watch room, and a ladder provided access to the lantern. Miniature lighthouses top the finials on the gallery railing, an architectural detail seen on very few lighthouses.

The keeper's house, painted white, stood about 50 feet north of the tower. The distinctive red oil house was built in 1902, and the walkway connecting the lighthouse to the keeper's house was added in 1911. The great blizzard of February 6–7, 1978, washed out the boathouse, which was replaced by the present structure.

The station originally had a fog bell operated by automatic striking machinery, with a cycle of two blows followed by an interval of 30 seconds, followed by a single blow and another 30-second pause. The bell's characteristic was later changed to a single blow every 30 seconds, and then in 1890 to a single blow every 15 seconds.

A white pyramidal tower replaced the original skeleton-frame bell tower in 1911. For a time, the keepers at Boon Island could hear the Nubble's 3,000-pound fog bell six miles away. A foghorn replaced the bell, and the bell tower was torn down in 1961.

The present fourth-order Fresnel lens, manufactured in 1891 by F. Barbier in Paris, is not the original one, but was moved from another station in 1928 after the original lens was damaged in an explosion. The original kerosene-fueled incandescent oil vapor lamp remained in use until the light was converted to electricity in 1938.

Leander White of New Castle, New Hampshire, was appointed keeper before the light went into service, but he was then assigned to Whaleback Light instead. Simon Leighton of York subsequently accepted the job, but he had to resign because of illness. Nathaniel H. Otterson of Hookset, New Hampshire, took over as keeper at the end of June 1879 at $500 yearly. Otterson was the cousin of New Hampshire's Governor Natt Head, a fact that apparently had a great deal to do with his appointment.

Soon after the light went into service, the *Portsmouth Chronicle* complained that it was no help to mariners entering York Harbor, although it did benefit vessels traveling along the coast. Coasting vessels had formerly steered for Boon Island Light, but now they could steer directly for the Nubble, meaning a more inside route and shorter voyages.

The lighthouse was a tourist attraction from the time it was built, and the keeper and his family immediately capitalized on the situation. An item in the August 7, 1880, issue of the *Portsmouth (NH) Journal* announced, "Visitors are not allowed to visit the lighthouse at York Nubble between the hours of 6 P.M. and 10 A.M.; but at other times the son of the keeper will row you over and back in his boat for ten cents."

Because so many people were visiting the island in summer, mishaps were not uncommon. In August 1889, it was reported that a Boston man slipped and fell, dislocating his shoulder. The injured man was rowed ashore by the keeper and was then taken to a doctor in Portsmouth. After treatment, he was "considerably shaken up, but merry as ever." In October 1892, a man who visited the Nubble to shoot waterfowl accidentally shot himself in the leg. Again, the keeper rowed him to the mainland for emergency medical help.

Otterson remained with his wife and son at the Nubble until the end of September 1885. His successor, Brackett Lewis of Kittery, Maine, formerly an assistant keeper at Whaleback Light, was in charge from

Cape Neddick Light Station circa early 1900s, with the original fog bell tower. *From the collection of the author.*

1885 to 1904, the longest stint of any keeper at the Nubble. While Lewis was keeper, his daughter, Hattie, wedded Charles Billings in the lantern room.

In 1898, a newspaper reported that Lewis had become so accustomed to the fog bell that he no longer heard it, and he often forgot to stop its operation after fog had cleared. In July of that year, it was recorded that the bell had been sounding for at least part of every day but two of the previous 30.

That same month, Lewis was ordered not to allow visitors on the island on Sundays. He had been charging 10 cents a trip to ferry visitors, and the authorities were apparently worried that the throngs of tourists on Sundays were interfering with his duties. Among the visitors spotted fishing from the island in June 1899 was Senator William E. Mason of Illinois.

The next keeper was William M. Brooks of Kittery, previously at Boon Island and White Island. Brooks and his wife had one son, who lived with an aunt in Portsmouth when school was in session and spent vacations at the light station. Toward the end of the Brooks's tenure, his son died of rheumatic fever at the Nubble at the age of 22.

Like Lewis before him, Brooks picked up extra cash by ferrying sightseers to the island. He also kept a supply of fishing gear and bait available on the island for visiting fishermen. Brooks's superiors noted that his ferry service allowed as many as "200 to 300 people at certain times to roam about the reservation with only the keeper's wife to care for the government property."

Rose Cushing Labrie, author of *Sentinel of the Sea: Nubble Light,* interviewed Brooks when he was in his 90s. He recalled that 10 cents was charged for round-trip ferry service to the island, and an additional five cents was charged for a tour of the station, led by his wife. The lighthouse authorities finally decided enough was enough, and Brooks "resigned" from lighthouse keeping in October 1912. He later operated the Bay View, a hotel at York Beach. During his retirement years in Kittery, Brooks was known as "Uncle Will" by his many friends.

After more than 25 years at the offshore stations on Boon Island and Burnt Island, Maine, and White Island, New Hampshire, James Burke of Portsmouth became keeper in 1912. One of his sons, Charles, was keeper at Wood Island Light, just up the coast off Biddeford Pool. James Burke had gone to sea at the age of 14 and eventually skippered fishing vessels before turning to lighthouse keeping. Like many lighthouse families, the Burkes kept a cow and chickens on the island. Burke went duck hunting and fishing to supplement his family's food supply. Lobsters, crabs, and mussels were also plentiful near the island.

James Burke was keeper 1912–19. *Courtesy of William O. Thomson.*

In a letter to the author Clifford Shattuck, James Burke's daughter Lucy Glidden Burke Steffen later recalled other details of life on the Nubble:

> We all had lots of work to do, as everything had to be immaculate throughout the house as well as the lighthouse tower. . . .
> We had lots of company, weather permitting. Many of my schoolmates used to enjoy coming over to the Nubble, some just to spend the day, some to spend the night or possibly to stay for a few days. Sometimes the sea got rough and they HAD to stay. We had an organ in the living room which I used to play and we all had such good times singing the old songs.

Our home was a very comfortable six-room house, having a very pleasant living room, a nice size dining room, a large kitchen with pantry, and three bedrooms upstairs. But, of course, no bathroom.

We had a large parlor stove which seemed to heat most of the house very well. Even though a severe storm might be blowing up outside, we were nice and cozy.

At low tide, it was sometimes possible to walk between the Nubble and the mainland. Lucy recalled being carried piggyback by her father, who would wear hip boots for the occasion, across the bar. She also recalled the large numbers of birds that would fly into the tower at night; the family sometimes had to rake up hundreds of them that lay dead on the ground in the morning.

James Burke's second wife died during his stay at the Nubble, and the government provided a lighthouse tender to transport the family to Boothbay Harbor for the funeral.

During World War I, the Burkes were joined on the Nubble by military personnel who kept watch for enemy submarines. The light was dimmed on some nights and extinguished on others, the intention being to confuse "possible submersibles."

After he retired in 1919, Burke opened a small fish and bait shop at York Beach. William Richardson, the next keeper, stayed until 1921. During his relatively brief stay, Richardson's son died of croup. Richardson was discharged for ferrying passengers to the Nubble for a fee.

Fairfield Moore was keeper 1921–28.
Courtesy of William O. Thomson.

Fairfield Moore, previously at Rockland Breakwater Light, was keeper from 1921 to 1928. The first birth of a child at the Nubble occurred on August 23, 1923, when Moore's daughter Phyllis Moore Searles delivered a baby girl.

In July 1926, it was reported that the fog bell tower was moved about four feet from its foundation by a powerful storm, leaving it on the brink of a precipice. Moore didn't dare sound the bell because he feared that the vibration could plunge the bell and tower into the sea. Repairs were soon completed.

On March 20, 1927, the keeper's daughter Eva Moore Kimball went into labor during a severe snowstorm. Keeper Moore rowed across the channel and picked up a local doctor. The two men returned to the Nubble just in time for the last seconds of the birth of Eva's daughter, Barbara.

Fairfield Moore returned to Rockland Breakwater Light in 1928 and was succeeded at the Nubble by Edmund Howe, who had previously been at Great Duck Island Light. During his tenure, Howe married his housekeeper, Emily Williams, in the living room of the keeper's house.

Unlike some of his predecessors, Howe wasn't eager to ferry would-be sightseers to the island. "Am I supposed to go ashore after everyone that comes down the bank and calls to me?" he wrote. "If I do I shan't get much chance to do anything else." The district superintendent responded by reassuring Howe that keepers had been "discharged from your station for transporting passengers to and from the station for hire."

Howe left in 1930 owing to ill health. After a very brief stint by Truman J. Lathrop, Eugene Coleman of Georgetown, Maine, became keeper following some time as first assistant at Boon Island. The keeper-powered ferry service was a thing of the past, but Coleman and his wife, Amanda, had plenty of visitors. The guest register showed totals of from 722 to 1092 visitors yearly between 1930 and 1934.

Eugene Coleman was the keeper at Cape Neddick Light 1930–43. With him is Sambo Tonkus, the station's famous cat. *Courtesy of William O. Thomson.*

The Burkes had left their family cat behind because he had become so attached to the Nubble, and the big tabby weighed 19 pounds by the time the Colemans arrived. Sambo Tonkus, also known as Mr. T, became well known to locals and tourists alike for his mousing and swimming prowess. Three or four times a day, he would swim to the mainland to hunt rodents hiding among the rocks.

During the Colemans' stay, the first indoor toilet was installed, and electricity came to the Nubble in 1938. During World War II, the light was extinguished and a lookout tower was built on the island. A contingent of Coast Guardsmen kept a 24-hour eye out for German U-boats. A U-boat sighted in 1943 just to the east of the Nubble was subsequently sunk by a depth charge southwest of Boon Island.

The historian Edward Rowe Snow, in his book *Famous New England Lighthouses,* wrote that on one occasion, Eugene Coleman was rowing across the channel near the Nubble with his wife, a friend, and a load of groceries, when the boat capsized. "The dory went over and the keeper had a busy five minutes, trying to rescue his wife, his friend, and the groceries," wrote Snow, "but all ended happily except for minor injuries to the groceries."

The Colemans moved on to Nauset Light on Cape Cod in 1943, and thereafter Coast Guard keepers staffed the Nubble. It remained a family station.

Elson Small was the keeper down the coast at Portsmouth Harbor Light, New Hampshire, from 1946 to 1948. On several occasions, he was called to substitute for the officer in charge at the Nubble. His wife, Connie, later recalled in her book, *The Lighthouse Keeper's Wife,* that she loved to have lunch on the porch at the Nubble, but she "felt like a goldfish in a bowl" as tourists watched her from across the channel.

The Coast Guard keeper from 1948 to 1951, Wilbur Brewster, had a parrot whose home was a cage in the living room. According to the lighthouse historian William O. Thomson, the parrot enjoyed carrying on conversations with visitors. Its favorite phrase was "I'll have a cup of coffee." Connie Small wrote that the bird loved to chatter along with her husband's banjo playing.

The usual way of getting to and from the Nubble was by boat. Coast Guard correspondence from the early 1950s shows that some consideration was given to the idea of a two-person aerial cable tramway between the mainland and the island, and a footbridge was also considered. Because of high costs and potential dangers, neither idea was pursued.

For a time, the keepers used a basket suspended on a line across the channel to transport supplies. Around 1967, one of the Coast Guard keepers, David Winchester, decided to save time and trouble by putting his two children in the basket each morning to send them on their way to school. A *Boston Globe* photographer snapped a picture of seven-year-old Ricky Winchester in the basket, and the photo appeared in newspapers across the country. After the district commander saw the photo in a Boston paper, an arrangement was made for the children to board on the mainland during the week. Soon after that, it became policy that families with school-age children were not sent to the Nubble.

Michael Hackett became the Coast Guard keeper in 1973. His wife, Sue, once called for someone to come and fix her Singer sewing machine. The repairman was to have been picked up in a boat by Michael, but he misunderstood the directions. A day late, the repairman showed up at the door—he had waited for low tide and walked across the channel.

The Hacketts also later recalled a man who phoned them at 2:00 a.m. to ask how the surfing conditions were near the lighthouse.

Russell Ahlgren, the last Coast Guard keeper, lived on the island with his wife, Brenda, and young son, Christopher, for 18 months before the 1987 automation of the station. The automation and destaffing were not well received by the people of York. William O. Thomson commented to the *Wall Street Journal,* "It's the biggest issue in our little town. I can't remember people getting so upset about anything since World War II broke out." The man installing the automation equipment, when asked what he was doing, avoided trouble by telling people onshore he was going out to fix the Ahlgrens' bathroom.

A crowd of more than 300 spectators witnessed the automation ceremonies on July 13, 1987, in a dense fog. Brenda Ahlgren wrote down her thoughts about leaving the island:

> *On our last night on the island we went for one last walk. We sat back on the rocks with Christopher between us and just watched the glow from that beautiful tall white tower and listened to the familiar drone of the horn we had come to enjoy. We felt that in its own special way the light was saying goodbye to family life on the island. As we sat there thinking back over our special adventure there was no way to hold back the tears.*

The Town of York was granted a 30-year lease to care for the station in 1989. In the same year, the town received a grant from the Maine Historic Preservation Commission for restoration work on the keeper's house. Two second-story windows were removed and replaced by a larger window that resembles the one originally installed. When the town took over, more than 300 unsolicited applications were received from people wanting to be live-in caretakers. The keeper's house remains unoccupied because of water and sewer issues.

In November 1997, the people of York voted overwhelmingly to allow the town's selectmen to "adopt" the lighthouse. Under the Maine Lights Program, coordinated by the Island Institute, the station officially became the property of the town in 1998. York's Parks and Recreation Department manages the site.

In 2001, the town installed a fire alarm system at Sohier Park and a new 120-foot ramp and dock on the Nubble. The foundation of the lighthouse was painted and regrouted, and the walkway to the lighthouse was replaced. More restoration of the buildings is needed. An April 2007 nor'easter damaged the keeper's house roof; both the island and Sohier Park sustained additional damage.

It's been estimated that 500,000 people visit Sohier Park annually to view the lighthouse. Director Mike Sullivan of York Parks and Recreation once said, "Part of the allure of Nubble Light is its mystical nature. You can't quite get there. You can almost reach it but you can't get there."

Sohier Park, incidentally, is named for William Davis Sohier, a lawyer from Boston who gave the land to the town in 1929. His father had bought the land for the fine duck hunting.

One of the most popular events of the year on the southern Maine coast is the annual Lighting of the Nubble, when the lighthouse and other buildings are illuminated with Christmas lights. The late November event is accompanied by holiday music and never fails to draw a

Cape Neddick Light with its annual holiday lighting. *Photo by the author.*

large crowd. The lighting has its roots in the early 1980s, when a volunteer, Margaret Cummings, donated some holiday lights in memory of her sister.

One of the Nubble's tireless volunteers, Verna Rundlett, later originated a Christmas-in-July event, which gives summer visitors a chance to view the station decorated just as it is at Christmastime. She also supervised the building of a welcome center at Sohier Park. The building, open seasonally, houses a gift shop and public restrooms.

The Nubble Light has probably appeared on more postcards, calendars, and other souvenirs than any other New England lighthouse, with the possible exception of Portland Head Light. In 1977, when NASA sent *Voyager II* into space to photograph the outer solar system, it was also loaded with artifacts designed to teach possible extraterrestrial civilizations about our planet. One of the images it carried was a picture of the Nubble Light.

For more information, or to help with the preservation of the Cape Neddick "Nubble" Light, contact the Friends of Nubble Light, 186 York Street, York, ME 03909; (207) 363-3078. In addition to the view from Sohier Park, the lighthouse can be seen from a seasonal excursion boat (the *Finestkind*) leaving Perkins Cove in Ogunquit. For information on Finestkind Cruises, visit www.finestkindcruises.com or call (207) 646-5227.

CHAPTER 4

Goat Island Light in October 2011. *Photo by the author.*

Goat Island Light

1833, 1859

In 1604, the French explorer Samuel de Champlain sailed along the Maine coast and passed by the area we now know as Cape Porpoise, part of the town of Kennebunkport. He accurately called the island-studded area Port aux Isles, or Island Harbor. A few years later, Capt. John Smith passed through and dubbed it Cape "Porpus" after a school of porpoises he saw cavorting nearby.

There's not really much of a cape, strictly speaking. The name came to include the village that later grew up around the harbor. Cape Porpoise was incorporated as a town in 1653. It was later depopulated by Indian depredations, but it was resettled in the early 1700s. The town was renamed Arundel in 1719, and renamed again as Kenne-bunkport in 1821. The old Cape Porpoise name now applies to the site of the original village and harbor, a locale that still retains its identity as a quiet fishing community.

Coastal and foreign trade developed at Cape Porpoise in the 1700s, its primary exports being lumber, fish, potash, and furs. There was some early shipbuilding in the harbor, but it never developed to the extent that it did on the Kennebunk River to the south. The fishing industry based in the harbor grew through the 1800s until, by the turn of the 20th century, Cape Porpoise boasted a fleet of nine schooners and many smaller vessels.

Goat Island, about three and a half acres in area, lies just east of the entrance to the harbor, about a mile from the mainland. The island was granted to Gregory Jeffreys in 1648 along with two of its island neigh-bors, and it passed through several owners before its government use.

The island figured in the American Revolution in 1782, when two British warships anchored close by and inflicted some damage on the area's shipping. The local militia gathered on Goat Island and fired on the British vessels, which soon retreated after heavy losses. Seventeen British soldiers died in the battle; one American was killed and one was wounded.

The approach to Cape Porpoise's harbor was always difficult. Its main channel is deep but narrow, and a dangerous ledge called Old Prince (marked today by a bell buoy) is about a quarter mile from the harbor's entrance, southeast of Goat Island. In March 1831, Congress appropriated $6,000 for a lighthouse on the island. A request for proposals was issued just before the end of the year by John Chandler, the local customs collector and lighthouse superintendent.

Newspapers announced that the station was nearly finished in July 1833, and it went into service in August. The conical rubblestone tower was only 20 feet tall. It was topped by an octagonal wrought-iron lantern, its light 38 feet above mean high water. The accompanying dwelling was also built of stone; it had three rooms on the first floor and three rooms on the small second floor. The first keeper was John Lord, of a prominent local family, at a salary of $350 per year. Lord remained keeper until 1841, when Thatcher Hutchins succeeded him.

The seminal report to Congress by the civil engineer I. W. P. Lewis in 1843 provides a portrait of a light station with many defects. Lewis described the tower as "laid up in lime mortar of bad quality, with a loose and leaky roof and decaying woodwork." The dwelling was no better: bad mortar, leaky roof and windows, and rotten cisterns. The east side of the house was built on uneven ground with no proper foundation, and the walls had cracked, rendering the room on the east side uninhabitable in winter. The well water was brackish and unfit for use.

Lewis saw the light as relatively unimportant; even with the light, the harbor was so difficult to access that it was rarely used as a harbor of refuge except out of dire necessity. Lewis believed a single lamp would have been sufficient for the station, instead of the seven that were then in use.

The keeper, Thatcher Hutchins, echoed Lewis's statements and added that leaks and condensation in the lantern required him to wipe the lantern glass three times in a night. He also mentioned that his predecessor, John Lord, had built a barn on the property, and Hutchins was paying Lord a rent of six dollars per year for use of the barn. Hutchins was provided a boat, but there was no boathouse on the island until 1905.

George Fletcher was keeper from 1846 to 1850. The station was inspected in August 1850, and the report noted that the tower and lantern were "in good order." The tower had recently been whitewashed inside and out, and the lantern and dome had been painted. The dwelling needed painting, but was otherwise in good order. The report concluded, "The keeper is a good one."

The Lighthouse Board announced in 1857 that the Goat Island Lighthouse was one of several in Maine that required rebuilding, and it was proposed that it be rebuilt "as rapidly as the means" would permit.

Funds were appropriated, and a new brick tower and dwelling were completed in 1859.

The cylindrical tower is 25 feet tall to the base of the octagonal iron lantern. A fifth-order Fresnel lens was installed. The new L-shaped, one-and-one-half-story, wood-frame keeper's house was attached to the tower by a covered walkway. The station's extant boathouse was added in 1905, and an oil house was built in 1907.

Dangerous ledges near the island continued to claim vessels, including 46 between 1865 and 1920. There was not a single death in all the wrecks, partly because the keepers at Goat Island picked up survivors near the island.

George Wakefield of Saco, Maine, kept the light from 1887 to 1921, the longest stint of any keeper at the station. Wakefield, who moon-lighted as a harbor pilot and fisherman, raised three children on the island with his wife, Mary (Tuman).

Late in Wakefield's tenure, in rough seas on the morning of New Year's Day, 1920, the three-masted schooners *George H. Trickey* and *Mary E. Olys* both ran into the rocks a stone's throw from the light-house. Wakefield immediately called the Coast Guard, but nothing could be done to save the schooners. Both vessels were pounded to pieces and were a total loss, but the crews escaped safely.

In his 1955 history of Cape Porpoise, Melville C. Freeman wrote that Wakefield was remembered "for his unusual care and watchfulness which saved lives because he was able to act quickly to bring rescue to sinking vessels." Wakefield died on the island in 1921. His daughter, Ethel, married Austin Lamont Sinnett, who later served as keeper.

James M. Anderson, formerly at Moose Peak, Matinicus Rock, and Cape Elizabeth, was keeper from 1926 to 1938, when he retired after 31 years of lighthouse life. In 1930, a schooner, the *Margery Austin*, went aground near the lighthouse, and Anderson went out in rough seas and helped refloat the vessel.

Anderson's daughter, Kathleen Stinson, went on to teach first grade for 43 years and retired in a house at Cape Porpoise. Asked what she liked best about lighthouse life, Stinson said, "It was the closeness of family, and you learned to live with one or two other families. I can't say I was fond of it, but I got along with everyone."

Joseph Bakken, a Coast Guard keeper who lived on Goat Island with his wife and three children, told the historian Edward Rowe Snow about his experience during a particularly severe storm in 1947. The waves washed over the island and damaged the walkway and the boat slip and ripped out a fence. In the commotion the family forgot about their dog and her newborn puppies. Later that night, Bakken went into the cellar and found several feet of water. Floating in the seawater was the box that contained the dog and her puppies. All were safe and sound and the keeper took them upstairs, out of harm's way.

The station's fog bell was replaced by a horn, sounding one blast every 20 seconds, in 1959. The Coast Guard initially planned to automate the station in 1976. Local residents felt that having a keeper on Goat Island was important to protect the island and light station from vandalism, as well as to keep an eye out for boaters in trouble. A petition drive convinced the Coast Guard to postpone automation.

Martin Cain, a Minnesota native, was the Coast Guard's officer in charge from October 1975 until June 1978. Cain monitored the local buoys and recorded the weather four times daily. He switched on the foghorn when a lighted buoy almost two miles away was obscured by fog or storm.

Cain lived on the island with his wife, Cathy, their baby, Martin J., and two cats and a dog. In a 1976 interview, he said he and his wife had to be more compatible than the average couple, but if they did have a fight, "One goes to one side of the island and the other goes to the other side and talks to the seagulls."

The Cains were on the island for the memorable blizzard of February 6–7, 1978, which folded the covered walkway between the house and tower "like an accordion" and swept it off the island. At the end of his stay, Cain said, "We've seen a lot out here and for the most part we've enjoyed it, but we're ready to leave."

Brad Culp, a Missouri native; his wife, Lisa; and their two children, Christian and Dakota, were Maine's last traditional lighthouse family. Christian was three when the Culps moved to the station in 1985, and he loved life on the island. There was a slight problem when he developed an interest in soccer, because the ball frequently ended up in the water. "You learned how to play defense very quickly," said Brad.

The Culps endured a major southeast gale in December 1986. Waves swept across the island, and a wooden walkway to the lighthouse was washed away. As another storm blew in a few weeks later, the Culps were ordered to evacuate. The motor on their little peapod boat died on the way to shore, but it finally restarted. A short time later, the station got a Boston Whaler with a bigger engine.

In the fall of 1990, Goat Island Light became the last lighthouse in Maine and one of the last in the United States to be automated. Its Fresnel lens was replaced by a modern 300-millimeter optic.

For a time during the presidency of George H. W. Bush, secret service agents lived at Goat Island, which offers a good vantage point of Bush's estate at Walker's Point. The island served as an air-sea

Scott Dombrowski of the Kennebunkport Conservation Trust in the lantern room of Goat Island Lighthouse in April 2006. *Photo by the author.*

command center, complete with a radar beacon.

In 1992, Goat Island was leased to the Kennebunkport Conservation Trust, which since its founding in 1973 has protected more than 600 acres of town land from development. In 1998, under the Maine Lights Program, the trust was awarded ownership of the property. In 2011, the fog bell tower and covered walkway were reconstructed as part of a $380,000 restoration project. The station's fog bell, long on display at the Kennebunkport Historical Society, was returned to the island and now hangs on the side of the tower.

For about eight years the caretaker on the island for most of the year was Dick Curtis. The 52-year-old Curtis died in a boating accident near the island in May 2002. He is deeply missed by the members of the Kennebunkport Conservation Trust and local residents.

Scott Dombrowski, the island overseer for the trust, spent some summers on the island with his wife, Karen, and their two sons, Eric and Gregory. Dombrowski has been decorating Goat Island Light with an elaborate display of Christmas lights every holiday season.

Kennebunkport and neighboring Kennebunk are popular tourist destinations that offer a variety of shops and historic homes. The lighthouse can be seen at a distance of about a half mile from the end of Pier Road in Cape Porpoise. Visitors with private boats are welcome on the island.

A modern LED-type optic was installed in 2008, and the light continues as an aid to navigation with a white flash every 6 seconds. For more information about the preservation of Goat Island Light, contact the Kennebunkport Conservation Trust, P.O. Box 7028, Cape Porpoise, ME 04014; www.the kennebunkportconservationtrust.org.

CHAPTER 5

Wood Island Light
in September 2005.
Photo by the author.

Wood Island Light

1808, 1839, 1858

Wood Island, about 35 acres in size, lies about two miles east of the entrance to the Saco River and less than a mile from the village known as Biddeford Pool. Biddeford Pool gets its name from a tidal inlet known simply as "The Pool," bounded by Fletcher's Neck to the south and Hills Beach to the north.

The communities of Saco and Biddeford grew up on the banks of the Saco River and around Winter Harbor at the river's mouth. The first sawmill in the area was established in 1653, and textile mills grew into the chief local industry. Fish and lumber were the other major exports.

Fletcher's Neck was considered a hazard to navigation, and Congress appropriated $5,000 for a lighthouse on Wood Island in March 1806. The government purchased land for the station from Pendleton Fletcher for $160. The purchase was made in two installments. The first sale included only some of the island's rocky shore, which was unsuitable for construction; a second transaction was necessary to obtain more suitable land. The seller was admired for his shrewdness in getting a double payment from Uncle Sam.

The light station was completed by September 1, 1807, for a sum of $4,750. The builders, Benjamin Beal and Duncan Thaxter, were subcontractors for Winslow Lewis. For reasons that aren't clear, the 45-foot octagonal wooden lighthouse wasn't put into service until the following year. A letter from a concerned party was printed in various newspapers in the spring of 1808, complaining, "From the completion of the light-house to this day, no light has ever shed its rays over a stormy sea; no vessel has found protection in it from a rocky shore; no pilot has discovered the entrance to Winter Harbour by its aid." The writer claimed that some mariners, thinking the light was in service, had mistaken other lights for it and narrowly escaped disaster as a result.

The first keeper, at a yearly salary of $225, was Benjamin Cole, who had been captain of a privateering vessel during the American Revolution. There were problems with the buildings from the start. The rubblestone dwelling was leaky; the walls were repointed with cement in 1832. The local customs collector and lighthouse superintendent, John Chandler, called the wooden tower "rotten" in 1835 and complained that it rocked in rough weather.

The 1808 tower lasted until 1839, when a new 44-foot conical rubblestone tower—20 feet in diameter at the base and 10 feet at the top—was built, along with a new one-story granite dwelling, after a congressional appropriation of $5,000 in July 1838. The revolving light was 69 feet above mean high water. A rotating "eclipser" created the appearance of a flash at certain intervals.

The engineer I. W. P. Lewis, in his 1843 report to Congress, wrote that the base of the tower rested on an uneven ledge, the walls were cracked and leaky, the mortar was bad, and the woodwork was decayed. Lewis described the lighting apparatus, which consisted of 10 lamps, each backed by a 13-inch reflector, arranged in two tiers. The entire apparatus revolved by means of a clockwork machine located below the floor of the lantern. The mechanism frequently stopped because of an accumulation of dirt and dust, which caused the light to become fixed and thereby easily mistaken for the light at Goat Island, a few miles to the southwest.

The one-and-one-half-story keeper's house was also in a deplorable state; the windows were leaky, the cellar had no floor and was wet and muddy, and the entire building was "very defective in materials and workmanship," according to Lewis. Jeremiah Berry of East Thomaston, who also built the 1827 lighthouse at Pemaquid Point, had built the dwelling.

John Adams, who had become keeper in 1841 at a yearly salary of $350, provided a statement for Lewis's report. He was provided a boat, but there was no landing place or shelter for it. Adams's predecessor, Abraham Norwood, had built a barn, fence, and stone wall; he demanded that Adams pay him $200 for the barn and 50 cents a rod for the wall and fence.

Norwood also had converted part of the dwelling into a "cowhouse" and pigsty. After Adams moved in, Norwood returned and harvested hay from the property, then charged the new keeper $14 per ton for hay that Adams needed to feed his cow. "This keeper," wrote Adams, "has since complained of me, because I decline buying the barn, walling, fencing, and other improvements."

Norwood disputed Adams's statements in a November 1843 letter, saying Adams had given a "wrong impression of the state of that light." Norwood claimed he had laid a floor in the cellar, and the dwelling didn't leak except for one window, which he had fixed. "I consider the tower strong and substantial," he wrote, "the dwelling house warm, tight, and comfortable, with an excellent cellar."

Keepers at a number of lighthouses, possibly under pressure from government officials, later disputed the negative statements made in

Wood Island Light Station circa 1860s. *U.S. Coast Guard.*

Lewis's report. The report, which found shoddy work throughout the country's lighthouse system, turned out to be accurate for the most part, which led to the formation of a new Lighthouse Board in 1852.

In 1856, the light was changed from white to red so it couldn't be confused with the lights to the north at Cape Elizabeth. The problems with the buildings continued; an 1850 inspection, when Stephen Bachelder was keeper, mentioned that the tower and dwelling were both still leaky. In August 1854, Congress appropriated $5,000 for another rebuilding of the tower.

The 1858 annual report of the Lighthouse Board announced that the work had been completed. A fourth-order Fresnel lens was installed in the 47-foot stone tower. The records for this work aren't clear, and it's possible that the tower was extensively renovated and not totally rebuilt. The present wood-frame keeper's house was also constructed at this time; it has undergone many modifications over the years.

Eben Emerson was keeper from 1861 to 1865. Emerson had been a sailor as a young man. He was said to be a staunch Republican and a dedicated abolitionist, and in his later years he was a beloved character known to all as "Uncle Eben."

At about 1:00 a.m. on March 16, 1865, Emerson rose from bed to trim the wick in the lighthouse lamp. Through thick fog and heavy surf, Emerson heard frantic voices out on the water. He tried to launch his boat toward the sounds, but the rough seas made it nearly impossible. The keeper raced to a nearby home on the island and recruited the help of the resident fisherman. The two men were able to launch the light station's small rowboat, and they soon encountered a brig that had run onto Washburn Ledge. The crewmen were clinging desperately to the rigging as the seas hammered the vessel.

Emerson managed to get aboard the brig. One lifeboat had already been lost, and another still hung by the davits. Emerson urged the men to climb into the lifeboat, while the captain remained at the bow and the mate stood by at the stern. Before returning to his rowboat, Emerson rescued two guinea pigs from belowdecks and put them in his pockets.

After returning to his boat, Emerson waited for a large wave and yelled, "Cut loose!" The lifeboat rode the wave and the crew escaped safely just before the brig, the *Edyth Ann* of Nova Scotia, was reduced to kindling by the surf. For his extraordinary heroism, Emerson was later awarded a plaque and a pair of binoculars from the Canadian government. After his lighthouse-keeping years, Emerson served as a deputy marshal in Biddeford.

Shipwrecks remained a regular occurrence in spite of the presence of the lighthouse. In 1872, the schooner *Cora Van Gilder* ran onto the rocks. When a volunteer lifesaving crew arrived, the captain told them his wife was ill with smallpox. Some of the lifesavers turned back out of fear of contracting the disease, but three continued with the rescue. The captain's wife spent time under the care of the keeper and his family, as well as a visiting doctor, and she eventually recovered.

Albert Norwood became keeper in 1872, and the following year Wood Island got its first fog signal, a 1,315-pound bell that sounded single and double blows, alternately, every 25 seconds. The striking machinery was housed in a pyramidal wooden tower. A new 1,200-pound bell was installed in 1890. For many years, the original bell was stuck unceremoniously upside down in the ground near the keeper's house and served as a flower planter.

Norwood retired in 1886. Thomas H. Orcutt, a veteran sea captain from Sedgwick, Maine, was keeper from 1886 until his death in 1905. Orcutt played a supporting role in the island's most infamous tragedy. The principals in the drama were Fred Milliken and Howard Hobbs.

Milliken, a fisherman, game warden, and special policeman in his 30s, lived in a house on Wood Island with his wife and three children for several years in the 1890s. He was described as a giant who easily carried his dory on his shoulders. Hobbs, a young fisherman, took up residence on the island, sharing a converted chicken house with another fisherman, William Moses. Both Hobbs and Moses were in their early 20s.

On June 2, 1896, Hobbs and Moses visited Old Orchard Beach, and they were reportedly intoxicated by the time they returned to Wood Island late in the afternoon. Milliken greeted them when they arrived, and he told Hobbs he wanted to speak to him—apparently about an overdue rent payment. Hobbs and Moses returned to their shack. Hobbs picked up his rifle, telling Moses he might shoot some birds. The two young men walked back to Milliken's property.

Milliken greeted Hobbs and Moses at his garden gate. Milliken asked if the rifle was loaded, and Hobbs replied that it wasn't. Milliken decided to check for himself. As he stepped toward Hobbs, the younger man fired a shot into Milliken's chest. Milliken's wife, who had been watching from the doorway, helped her husband inside and onto a bed. Moses left with Milliken's young stepson to row ashore with the intention of fetching a doctor. Milliken died within 45 minutes. In a daze, Hobbs went to the keeper's dwelling at the lighthouse, where Orcutt advised him to give himself up to the authorities. Hobbs returned to his small shack and proceeded to put a bullet in his own head.

Some people have claimed the island is cursed. Another incident that contributed to this idea was the suicide of another fisherman;

Keeper Thomas Orcutt with Sailor, his famous bell-ringing dog. *Courtesy of the Friends of Wood Island Lighthouse.*

after years of solitary island existence, the man went to a hotel in Saco and jumped from a window.

Robert Thayer Sterling, in *Lighthouses of the Maine Coast and the Men Who Keep Them,* described another strange incident. Sometime in the late 1800s, a Frenchman who lived on the west side of the island was selling liquor to visiting fishermen. Brawls among the fishermen became commonplace on the island. One of the fights got out of hand, and a drunken fisherman set fire to the Frenchman's shack. According to Sterling, "The bottles broke and the seething alcoholic blue flames created such a torchlight that it was seen twenty miles at sea."

In addition to Wood Island's macabre history, there's also a brighter tradition of fascinating pets. Orcutt's dog, Sailor, a mostly black mongrel (described as a Scotch collie in one article), was taken to the island as a two-month-old puppy and went on to achieve wide fame. In 1894, the *Lewiston (ME) Journal* reported:

> *It is customary for passing steamers to salute the light and the keeper returns it by ringing the bell. The other day a tug whistled three times. The Captain did not hear it, but the dog did. He ran to the door and tried to attract the Captain's attention by howling. Failing to do this he ran away and then came a second time with no better result. Then he decided to attend to the matter himself, so he seized the rope, which hangs outside, between his teeth and began to ring the bell.*

The self-trained Sailor developed the habit of vigorously ringing the bell for every passing vessel. Over the next few years, many passengers aboard local excursion steamers were startled to see the dog's amazing performances. Sailor was said to possess almost human intelligence. He also served as a messenger, delighting in carrying letters and other small articles in his mouth. It was claimed that he understood all that was said to him. In 1900, Orcutt remarked: "Sailor and I are old comrades. Wood Island would indeed be a lonely place if I hadn't the dog to keep me company. He is a bright, intelligent companion and is perfectly content to live the life of a lighthouse keeper away from all dog friends."

Orcutt died after a brief illness in 1905 at the age of 73. His beloved Sailor had died in his arms just a few months earlier. Orcutt was "well known among the sea faring men and was well liked by all," according to an obituary. His son-in-law, Levi Jeffers, filled in as keeper until a new one could be appointed.

Charles A. Burke, who stayed until 1914, next filled the post. In October 1906, several earthquake shocks shook the area. Burke told

Earle Benson was keeper 1934–52. *Courtesy of the American Lighthouse Foundation.*

mainland residents that the island rocked "like the shaking of gelatin pudding" during one of the shocks, but no damage was done.

The last U.S. Lighthouse Service keeper at Wood Island Light was Earle Benson, a veteran of World War I who took over when George E. Woodward was transferred in 1934. Benson and his wife, Alice, loved Wood Island the most of their four stations. After a stint at Portland Head Light, where a constant flow of tourists was the norm, the Bensons preferred the quiet of Wood Island. Benson joined the Coast Guard when it took over the Lighthouse Service in 1939; he became a chief boatswain's mate and stayed on the island until 1952.

The Coast Guard converted the light station to electricity in 1950. The Bensons were thrilled to replace their battery-operated radio with a television. Their TV watching included the 1950 World Series. "It was so clear you could see the lines on the ball," said Benson. The Bensons' favorite TV show was *The Lone Ranger.* Also in 1950, the Coast Guard drilled for freshwater, and a new pump house with an electric pump was installed on the island.

Wood Island remained a family station under the Coast Guard. Edward G. Frank succeeded Benson as officer in charge in January 1952. Frank moved to the island with his wife, Eloise; a son, Steven, was born that April. The Franks' daughter, Michele, lived with her grandmother in Vermont to attend school and lived on Wood Island during school vacations.

The Frank family, like many of their predecessors, kept chickens at the station. They also had several pets: a St. Bernard named Henry, a cocker spaniel named Crissey, a Maine coon cat named Timmy, and another cat named Tom. Once, when it seemed that all the chickens had disappeared, Crissey was able to find them in their hiding places in the rocks.

In the 1950s, the lens still revolved by means of a clockwork mechanism that had to be rewound every few hours in times of fog. Frank wound the mechanism at 11:30 p.m., meaning it had to be wound again in the early morning. Michele later recalled that she often earned a quarter by rising before dawn to do the winding. Sometimes she would strike the bell manually, by pulling a rope, while her father rewound the machine.

Laurier Burnham, a native of Biddeford, was the keeper for the Coast Guard from 1959 to 1963. He was a central figure in one of the island's greatest dramas. On November 29, 1960, Burnham's two-year-old daughter, Tammy, was seriously ill. The seas were growing increasingly rough that late afternoon, and a 30-foot boat with a four-man crew was dispatched from the nearby Coast Guard station at Fletcher's Neck to take Tammy to the mainland for medical attention. The boat anchored near the island and two 19-year-old crewmen approached the island in a skiff.

Burnham handed his daughter to the men in the skiff, and they started back for the larger boat. A sudden wave capsized the skiff, throwing its three occupants into the turbulent water. By this time, it was so dark that neither Burnham nor the Coast Guardsmen on the 30-footer were able to see what had happened to the skiff. One of the men from the skiff managed to swim back to the larger boat. The other man, Edward Syvinski, clung firmly to Tammy even as they were pulled underwater several times. He managed to swim with the girl to a nearby island.

Burnham had been ordered to remain at the light station, but he was aware of the situation and decided to take matters into his own hands. He ventured into the dark and stormy seas in his little peapod boat to search for his daughter. He eventually found Syvinski and his daughter and got both into his boat. He transported them safely to the 30-footer, and Tammy was rushed to shore. She was taken to a hospital, where she fully recovered from her illness.

In 1993, 33 years after the dramatic incident, the Coast Guard awarded Commendation Medals to Burnham and Syvinski. It was determined that a lobsterman, Preston Alley, had helped in the rescue, and his widow was presented a medal as well. Laurier Burnham also served at Halfway Rock Lighthouse and on several lightships during his Coast Guard career. When he died in 1997, his wife recalled, "My husband was very safety conscious. He really knew how to handle a boat."

David Winchester of the Coast Guard, in charge in 1963–64, and his family got only two days ashore each month, but they stayed in touch with the mainland through weekly visits from the mailboat. Just before Christmas in 1963, Winchester bought a Christmas tree on the mainland, took it back to the island in a boat, and hauled it across the island's half-mile boardwalk from the boathouse to the keeper's house using a tractor and cart.

Jim Roche was the Coast Guard keeper in the late 1960s. A Brooklyn, New York, native, Roche told a reporter that he was "converted to Maine." Roche shared the keeper's house with his wife, Pat, two small children (a third was born in 1969), three dogs, and three cats. "There's nothing better for real family living than an island," said Pat.

Under the Roches, the keeper's house became a makeshift wildlife hospital. A sick duck spent a week recuperating in the bathtub, and a seagull with a broken wing was nursed back to health. The gull would eat only pork chops, and only when Pat wore a fur coat. "Maybe it thought I was its mother," she said.

By the 1970s, many improvements were made to the keeper's house. There were three bedrooms, a kitchen, an office, a living room, laundry room, and an upstairs bathroom. The furnace in the basement was converted from coal to oil in the 1950s. Water from a freshwater well was pumped into a 2,000-gallon cistern and then pumped to the faucets as needed.

The Coast Guard keeper from 1970 to 1972 was Cliff Trebilcock. In an interview years later, he recalled a time when one of his sons was ill and in need of penicillin during a bad storm. Trebilcock found a local lobsterman who was willing to pick up the medicine and bring it back to the island. When the lobsterman returned, the seas were too rough to land his boat. He put the medicine into an empty peanut butter jar and floated it inside a life preserver, and Trebilcock was able to pull it in with a boat hook after several tries.

Jerry Murray, the Coast Guard officer in charge from 1973 to 1976, had always wanted to be a lighthouse keeper, so his assignment to Wood Island was a dream come true. There were hardships, such as when he and his family had to stay on the island for three months because of rough weather, but the island life had its rewards. "To experience the pleasure of living on your own island, surrounded on three sides with a view of open sea and the most glorious sunrises you can imagine, is great," said Susan Murray, Jerry's wife. The biggest inconvenience, she said, was the finicky electric toilet.

According to the booklet *The Animals of Wood Island* by Donna Goulding, the Murrays had a rooster that thought he was a seagull.

The rooster, a Rhode Island Red named Gregory Peck, would fly about 200 yards with the gulls before he'd drop back to earth. Undaunted, he kept trying.

Mike McQuade and his wife, Patsy, both natives of Omaha, Nebraska, followed the Murrays on Wood Island. McQuade had asked for lighthouse duty, and he was pleased with the assignment. "We couldn't have asked for a better place to be near the ocean," he said. In addition to operating the light, McQuade was required to turn on the station's fog signal when the visibility dropped to less than two and a half miles, and he also had to keep an eye on 20 navigational buoys near the island.

The McQuades inherited the station's mascot, a five-year-old collie named Kelly. Kelly came to Wood Island Light as a puppy and performed the important duty of keeping rats and mice under control. The McQuades also brought along Torrey, their Lhasa apso. In 1978, the McQuades welcomed their first child, Damian, born on the mainland at Webber Hospital in Biddeford.

In the late 1960s, Wood Island Light's lantern was removed and a rotating aerobeacon was installed. The public complained about the strange-looking "headless" lighthouse, so a new welded aluminum lantern was fabricated and installed when the light was automated and the last Coast Guard keeper and his family were removed in 1986.

Sheri Poftak, historian for the Friends of Wood Island Lighthouse. *Photo by the author.*

The island was briefly considered a possible site for a nuclear power plant in the late 1960s. Then, in 1970, 28 of the island's 35 acres were deeded to the Maine Audubon Society. The society manages most of the island, apart from the light station.

Considering the island's history of shipwrecks and tragedy, it's probably no surprise that there have also been tales of ghostly hauntings. Members of the New England Ghost Project ventured to the island for two overnight investigations in 2005 and 2006. The intriguing results included photos of what seems to be the apparition of a woman in the basement of the keeper's house.

In early 2003, a chapter of the American Lighthouse Foundation was formed to care for the light station. The group, Friends of Wood Island Lighthouse, also takes care of the wooden boardwalk from the boathouse to the keeper's house and seven acres of land at the light station. In the fall of 2009, FOWIL contracted Stone Age Masonry to carry out the restoration of the lighthouse tower. The work was completed in the summer of 2010. The exterior of the keeper's house was restored by Leslie Masonry in 2011. The $200,000 project included the restoration of the porch to its 1906 design. The covered walkway between the house and tower was restored in 2012.

Wood Island Light, still an active aid to navigation, can be seen from a walking trail along the water at the East Point Audubon Sanctuary in Biddeford Pool. It's about a 15-minute walk from the start of the trail to a view of the lighthouse.

The station's original fog bell, manufactured in 1872 by Vickers, Sons & Company in England, is now on display at Vines Landing in Biddeford Pool.

In the summer season, boat tours are offered to the island and light station from Vines Landing in Biddeford Pool. The tours take about 90 minutes, and members of Friends of Wood Island Lighthouse get priority for reservations. Visit www.woodislandlighthouse.org for the current schedule and other information, or call (207) 286-3229 or contact Friends of Wood Island Lighthouse, P. O. Box 26, Biddeford Pool, ME 04006.

CHAPTER 6

Cape Elizabeth Light in 2002.
Photo by the author.

Cape Elizabeth Light

(Cape Elizabeth Two Lights)
1828, 1874

When the English explorer Capt. John Smith sailed along the coast of New England in 1614, he named a prominent cape in what is now southern Maine after Princess Elizabeth, sister of Charles I. Two-hundred-acre Richmond Island, a short distance off Cape Elizabeth to the south, was the site of the earliest European settlement in this part of Maine, beginning in 1628. The settlement that later developed on the cape was, for many years, part of the town of Falmouth.

Cape Elizabeth was incorporated as a separate town in 1765. In 1895, the northern half of the town was incorporated as South Portland. It was the development of Portland Harbor, along the north side of the cape on the Fore River, that led to the need for better aids to navigation in the vicinity. The harbor rebounded after the Revolution to become the most important seaport in the state.

The approach to Portland Harbor from the south was treacherous, and as maritime trade increased, so did shipwrecks. One of the most heartrending near Cape Elizabeth was the July 12, 1807, wreck of the schooner *Charles,* which was dashed to pieces on a reef in fog and heavy seas. At least 16 men and women died in the disaster.

A 50-foot black and white pyramidal stone day beacon was erected in 1811 on a rocky promontory at the southeastern point of Cape Elizabeth, at the southwestern limit of Casco Bay and about five miles southeast of Portland Harbor. The beacon was completed by the end of November by the contractors Edward Robinson and John F. Bartlett.

Shipping in the vicinity continued to increase, and officials recognized the need for a light station. Stephen Pleasonton, the Treasury official in charge of the nation's lighthouses, wrote to Isaac Ilsley, the superintendent of Maine's lighthouses, in March 1827, requesting that Ilsley "make an examination, or cause it to be made" and to inform Pleasonton whether one or two lighthouses were necessary, and what they would cost.

A sum of $4,500 was appropriated in February 1828. It was determined that the station would have two lights, one fixed and one revolving, to differentiate it from Wood Island Light (revolving) to the south, and from Portland Head Light (fixed) to the north.

The west tower at Cape Elizabeth, circa 1859. *National Archives.*

The stone marker was torn down to make way for the first pair of Cape Elizabeth lighthouses, built by the mason Jeremiah Berry for $4,250. Ilsley visited the site to keep an eye on the construction, and he later requested reimbursement for his own expenses. The frugal Pleasonton refused, telling Ilsley to "strike out of the account . . . the charge for superintendence of the workmen."

The station was established on 12 acres of land bought from three local men for $50. The east light was built on the former site of the marker, and the inner or west light was built directly to the west, 895 feet away. They were the second set of twin lighthouses on the Maine coast, coming a short time after the pair at Matinicus Rock.

Both 65-foot towers (to the tops of the lanterns) were octagonal and built of rubblestone, with octagonal wrought-iron lanterns. The east tower had 15 lamps with 16-inch reflectors, showing a fixed white light 129 feet above mean high water. The west tower had 14 lamps with 14-inch reflectors; the apparatus revolved to produce a flashing light, 132 feet above mean high water. The lights were in service by the end of October 1828.

The lights were considered among the most important on the coast; mariners approaching Portland Harbor would line them up to know they were on course. Elisha Jordan was appointed the first keeper—from a field of 18 men—at a salary of $450 per year, and he remained for six years. Jordan was instructed that he had to "reside at the station and make it a habit to be at home."

Problems with the construction of the towers were reported as early as November 1829, when John Chandler, the customs collector and local lighthouse superintendent, wrote to Stephen Pleasonton. "The Light Houses which were built a year or two since on Cape Elizabeth never did dry," wrote Chandler. "They were built so late in the season that the mortar froze, and whenever rain came, it ran amongst the stone and kept it continually wet."

Jordan lost his keeper's position for political reasons in 1834. His successor, Charles Staples, was one of the men who had sold land for the light station to the government. Staples served only a brief time before dying of cancer in 1835. During his stay, the station got its first fog bell, rung by means of striking machinery housed in a 20-foot tower. The keeper was subsequently awarded a $50 raise to his yearly salary because of the extra duties associated with the bell.

In his 1843 report to Congress, the civil engineer I. W. P. Lewis was very critical of the construction of the towers. The mortar was bad, and the roofs and walls were leaky. The machine that rotated the light in the west tower was defective and frequently stopped. The stone dwelling, consisting of two rooms and an attached kitchen on the first floor and two small rooms upstairs, was also badly built and leaky. Lewis reported additionally that the fog bell could not be heard above the roar of the surf.

George Fickett, who had been keeper since 1841 at a yearly salary of $500, provided a statement for Lewis's report, corroborating his description of the poor state of the buildings. Fickett had paid $150 to

The east tower at Cape Elizabeth, circa 1859. *U.S. Coast Guard.*

his predecessor for a barn and other outbuildings at the station. He complained that the great distance between the two towers made his work arduous, especially when snow filled the valley between them.

In November 1843, Fickett recanted some of the statements he had given Lewis, possibly under pressure from government officials. He adding the following: "I have heard seamen speak of these lights as excellent ones. . . . The light-houses had not been repaired not even whitewashed for two years, when Mr. Lewis visited them; and the repairs were delayed that year, for Mr. Lewis to inspect them first, so that he could see them in their worst state, and all defects, if any, should be visible."

Hiram Staples followed Fickett as keeper in 1844. During his tenure, it was recorded that the poet Henry Wadsworth Longfellow, who lived in Portland, visited the station in 1847 and climbed the west tower.

William Jordan, who became keeper in July 1849, had no previous experience, and Staples had to train him before he departed. A new lantern was installed on the west tower in 1850, along with new lighting apparatus. An inspection report that year revealed that the towers and dwelling were still leaky, and the bell machinery needed repair.

Congress passed legislation in March 1851 authorizing the formation of the Lighthouse Board, under the Treasury Department, to be composed of two officers of the navy, two officers of the army, a "civil officer of high scientific attainment," and a junior officer of the navy to act as secretary. Representatives of the board quickly set out to examine a number of light stations that were "characteristic and afforded the best specimens of the several kinds." The Cape Elizabeth station was examined on July 4, 1851.

The report described the poor condition of the buildings; the east tower was damp inside, and the walls were discolored and cracked. Both towers were "pretty well built, but greatly neglected." As I. W. P. Lewis had pointed out almost a decade earlier, even with a light wind the fog bell could be heard no farther than the nearby beach. The report also recommended that the station be assigned at least one assistant, so that someone could be on watch during the entire night.

Keeper Jordan complained of the lack of assistants in an 1852 letter. "I have to hire a boy during the summer season," he wrote, "and a man during the winter months, and, if I did not do so, could not faithfully keep things in order." The yearly salary of the keeper was still $500; Jordan asked for a raise of $100 to cover the expense of hiring extra help. Nathan Davis succeeded Jordan as keeper in 1853, and Davis was provided an assistant at $200 yearly. A second assistant was added a few years later.

In 1853, J. B. Coyle of the Portland Steam Packet Company wrote to the local lighthouse superintendent, complaining that the fog bell was "entirely too small for one occupying so important position." At a cost of $2,500, a larger bell and new striking machinery were installed the following year. By the end of 1854, the towers got new cast-iron stairways, and both were lined with brick. Fresnel lenses were installed in the towers around the same time, replacing the old multiple lamps and reflectors.

In the summer of 1855, it was announced that the west light was to be discontinued, and the characteristic of the east light would be changed to occulting. Despite protests, the change went into effect on August 1, 1855. Under this arrangement, the single revolving light was often hard to distinguish from Wood Island Light to the south. On April 1, 1856, the two lights were returned to their former condition, and the light at Wood Island was changed from white to red to eliminate any chance of confusion.

During the Civil War, Asbury Staples, the assistant keeper in charge of the west light, enlisted in the Second Maine Battery Light Artillery. His father, Michael Staples, who was also an assistant keeper, requested that his other children be officially appointed assistants. His teenaged daughter Amelia and her younger brother, Charles, became responsible for keeping the light and related equipment. Amelia and Charles assisted in the grim task of draping the towers in black at the news of President Lincoln's assassination.

The towers were repainted in 1865 in an effort to make them easier to recognize in the daytime. The west tower received one large vertical red stripe, and the east tower was painted with four horizontal red bands.

The Lighthouse Board announced that a steam fog whistle with a powerful eight-second blast was installed in 1869, and a new building was constructed to house the equipment. Two more assistant keepers were assigned to the station at this time. A more powerful fog whistle was installed by 1876.

A larger brick fog signal building, 32 by 32 feet, was constructed in 1886. The fog signal was in operation for 1,117 hours in 1888, which consumed 71,500 pounds of coal.

In 1872, the Lighthouse Board announced that the two towers had deteriorated to the point that they had to be rebuilt. A pair of identical 67-foot cast-iron towers replaced the original towers in 1874, after a congressional appropriation of $30,000. The cast-iron segments of the towers were manufactured at the Portland Machine Works. The lighthouses were given delicate Italianate architectural detailing. There were windows on the east and west sides at the first, third, and fifth levels, and the watch rooms, at the sixth level, were each surrounded by a circular gallery. Second-order Fresnel lenses were installed in both towers. A new wood-frame, one-and-one-half-story dwelling was built for the principal keeper near the east tower in 1878.

Marcus Aurelius Hanna, the best-known keeper in this station's history, was born in 1842 while his father, James Tolman Hanna, was keeper of Franklin Island Light. His grandfather had been one of the first keepers of Boon Island Light.

Marcus Hanna went to sea as a cabin boy at the age of 10. During his service in the Civil War, he was praised for exposing himself to enemy fire while retrieving water for his men, an action that later earned him the Medal of Honor. After serving as keeper at Pemaquid Point beginning in 1869, Hanna became the principal keeper at Cape Elizabeth in 1873. His father served as an assistant keeper at the station from 1853 to 1876, and his brothers, William Henry and Nathaniel John, served stints as assistant keepers in the 1870s.

On the night of January 28, 1885, Marcus Hanna was suffering from a bad cold. A storm hit and increased in severity as the night progressed. Hanna sounded the steam fog whistle all night despite being ill and exhausted. Hiram Staples, the assistant keeper, relieved Hanna at 6:00 a.m. The blizzard was by then "one of the coldest and most violent storms of snow, wind and vapor . . . that I ever witnessed," Hanna later said. He had to crawl through enormous snowdrifts back to the house.

Marcus Hanna, lighthouse keeper and Medal of Honor recipient. *U.S. Coast Guard.*

Hanna was soon asleep. His wife, Louise (Davis), who held one of the assistant keeper positions for some years, extinguished the lights in both towers after sunrise. Then, at 8:40 a.m., she looked out toward the ocean and saw a schooner aground on Dyer's Ledge, near the fog signal building. The vessel was the *Australia* out of Boothbay, which had been headed for Boston with a cargo of ice from the Kennebec

Early-1900s postcard image of the east tower and keeper's house. *From the collection of the author.*

River in the hold and 150 barrels of mackerel on deck. The captain had already been swept away by the waves; only two crew members remained alive. The men had climbed to the rigging and were practically frozen alive in the bitter cold.

Louise Hanna shouted to her husband, informing him that a vessel was ashore. The keeper rushed to the signal house. Staples hadn't seen the wreck through the thick snow. The two men hurried to the edge of the water near the schooner. Hanna later recalled, "I felt a terrible responsibility thrust upon me, and I resolved to attempt the rescue at any hazard." He tried a number of times to throw a line to the vessel but failed. Staples returned to the fog signal building. Meanwhile, Hanna's wife alerted neighbors.

Hanna, practically frozen by this time, waded waist-deep into the ocean and again threw a line to the schooner, this time hitting his target. One of the crewmen, Irving Pierce, managed to pull himself from the rigging and tied the line around himself. Hanna somehow pulled the helpless man through the waves and over the rocks to the shore. According to Hanna, "Pierce's jaws were set; he was totally blind from exposure to the cold, and the expression of his face I shall not soon forget."

After several tries, Hanna landed the line on the *Australia* again. The other crewman, William Kellar, tied the rope around himself. Hanna's strength was giving out and he faltered as he tried to pull the man to safety. Just then, Staples and two neighbors arrived. The four men hauled Kellar to the shore, and then carried the two sailors to the fog signal building. The men were given dry clothes and, once they had thawed enough, hot food and drink. After two days they had recovered enough to be taken to Portland by sled.

Six months later, Marcus Hanna received a gold lifesaving medal for "heroism involving great peril to his life," in recognition of one of the greatest lifesaving feats at an American lighthouse. (In August 1997, the Coast Guard launched a new $12.5-million, 175-foot buoy tender named the *Marcus Hanna*. A replica of Hanna's lifesaving medal is mounted on board. The cutter's home port is South Portland, Maine.)

The Hannas left in 1888, and Leander White of New Castle, New Hampshire, became the new principal keeper. White stayed until 1909, when he became the keeper at Portsmouth Harbor Light Station in New Hampshire. When he left Cape Elizabeth, a newspaper called *Coast Watch* reported: "Capt. White is the fourth oldest keeper in point of service in this district, having served 37 years in the lighthouse dept. He is one of the best men in this dept. of the government."

In 1890, the old stone dwelling occupied by the second assistant keeper was torn down, and a new wood-frame dwelling was constructed. The Lighthouse Board announced in 1891 that four families were living in three houses, two near the east tower and one near the west tower. A fourth dwelling, said the board, was urgently needed. No action was taken until 1901, when the residence at the west tower was enlarged and improved.

The west light was discontinued again in 1882; again it was relighted after complaints. The towers were painted brown during two separate periods; they have been white since 1902, when the keeper and his three assistants painted them.

Frank Lewis Cotton, formerly an assistant at Spring Point Ledge Light and Petit Manan Light, was an assistant keeper and then principal keeper from 1909 to 1926. In 1912, the government started a practice of awarding an "efficiency flag" to the best-kept light station in each district. Cotton and his assistants at Cape Elizabeth had the honor of being the first recipients of this award in the First District.

During World War I, military personnel patrolled the grounds around the station. One of the assistant keepers at the time was James Anderson, and his daughter, Edwina Davis, later recalled that the soldiers swept off a pond so the lighthouse families could ice skate. Edwina and the other lighthouse children walked four miles each way to school every day, as there was no other way for them to get there.

In 1924, government officials decided to change the station to a single light, and the west light was extinguished for good on June 14.

On December 20, 1925, the east light was electrified and increased to 500,000 candlepower, which at the time made it the second most powerful light in New England (after Highland Light on Cape Cod).

When a powerful new foghorn replaced the old steam whistle in 1929, not everyone was pleased. A local man wrote to the local lighthouse superintendent, Capt. C. E. Sherman, complaining that the new horn had "a blast that is very penetrating and at night very annoying." Capt. Sherman replied that the new signal shouldn't be any more annoying than the old one, once people got used to it. He added that the new horn had been deemed "very satisfactory to not only the fishermen but to all vessels entering and leaving Portland Harbor."

One evening in January 1934, Keeper Joseph H. Upton, 65 years old, went to the tower at about 9:30 to light an auxiliary light in place of the main light in the east tower, which had failed. A couple of hours later, his wife went to the tower and found Upton unconscious at the bottom of the stairs. A fall down the stairs had fractured his skull, and he died in a hospital a short time later. Upton, a native of Cape Elizabeth and a former ferry captain, had previously been keeper at White Island Light in New Hampshire and assistant keeper at Matinicus Rock. He had been in charge at Cape Elizabeth since 1926.

The last civilian keeper at Cape Elizabeth was Capt. Edward Elliot. During World War II, Elliot was ordered to extinguish the light during a coastal blackout. The keeper also owned a nearby cottage that he rented to a woman who often complained about the lighthouse beam disturbing her sleep. On the night he was ordered to turn off the light, Elliot visited the woman and told her he had decided to turn it off so she could sleep better. It wasn't until she read the newspaper that the tenant realized Elliot had been joking.

One of the famous wrecks near Two Lights was the collier *Oakey L. Alexander* in 1947. The 395-foot vessel broke in two eight miles from Cape Elizabeth in a March gale. The stern half, with 32 crew members aboard, drifted onto the rocks near the light station. Earle Drinkwater and his crew at the nearby Cape Elizabeth Lifeboat Station, with help from other Coast Guardsmen and local fishermen, rescued the entire crew by breeches buoy (a single-person rescue device consisting of canvas breeches attached to a ring buoy suspended from a pulley running along a rope from ship to shore). The wrecked *Alexander* remained just offshore at Cape Elizabeth for years and was viewed by countless sightseers.

Coast Guardsman Clifton Morong spent about nine years on the crew at the light station. He had been born in the keeper's house by the east tower while his father, Alonzo Morong, was an assistant keeper. Shortly after Clifton Morong's arrival, in 1946, the crew at the lighthouse was consolidated with the crew at the Cape Elizabeth Lifeboat Station at the foot of the hill near the lighthouse.

Morong's wife, Shirley, in an article for *Lighthouse Digest*, recalled Hurricane Carol, which struck on August 31, 1954. "Electric power was off," she wrote, "trees were being uprooted, and seas were pounding the shore and a lot of damage [was] done all over New England. I was at the house alone at Two Lights and was quite nervous when the front screen door blew off." The station weathered the storm with no major damage.

Once, when the revolving mechanism for the lens stopped working, Morong's uncle Fred Morong, who for many years was the district machinist, was called in from the Coast Guard station at South Portland. He soon had the mechanism performing properly. In addition to his prowess as a technician, Fred Morong dabbled in poetry. His poem "Brasswork" was published in Robert Thayer Sterling's book *Lighthouses of the Maine Coast and the Men Who Keep Them* in 1935, and it became one of the best-known poems related to lighthouse keeping. The poem, a lightkeeper's lament about the endless job of polishing the omnipresent brasswork, includes these verses:

> *The devil himself could never invent,*
> *A material causing more world wide lament,*
> *And in Uncle Sam's service about ninety percent*
> *Is BRASSWORK*
>
> *And when I have polished until I am cold,*
> *And I have taken my oath to the Heavenly fold,*
> *Will my harp and my crown be made of pure gold?*
> *No! BRASSWORK*

Another keeper during the Coast Guard era was Joseph Bakken, the son of a Lighthouse Service keeper. A strange item appeared in newspapers in a "Word from the Wickies" column in 1953. Bakken's wife reported that the lighthouse mascot, a five-month-old alligator from Louisiana, had disappeared. "If anyone sees a stray alligator around," she wrote, "you'll know where it came from."

During World War II, the lantern was removed from the discontinued west light, and the tower was converted into an observation post. After its military use in World War II, the west tower passed into private ownership. It was sold to the highest bidder in 1959, along with several buildings and 10½ acres of land.

The famed American artist Edward Hopper immortalized the east light in the 1920s in several of his paintings. One of the paintings was reproduced on a 1970 postage stamp commemorating the 150th anniversary of Maine's statehood.

In 1971, the actor Gary Merrill (Bette Davis's ex-husband) purchased the west tower for $28,000. Merrill, a Connecticut native, had come to know the Maine coast as a boy when he stayed at his grandmother's home at Prouts Neck. "How can anyone not be taken by the idea of living in a lighthouse?" he asked a writer for *Yankee* magazine.

Merrill announced plans to turn the tower into a year-round home, telling a reporter that he preferred Maine to Hollywood. "It's death out there," he said. "In Maine, I live with the squirrels and forget about it." During his time at Cape Elizabeth, Merrill was regarded as an eccentric. Among other things, he gained attention by putting a donkey in the back of his Cadillac convertible and driving through town. He once ran unsuccessfully for the Maine state legislature, and in 1974 he announced his intention to run for president. Merrill sold the property in 1983, and a new house was later built next to the tower.

The east light was automated in 1963, and its 1,800-pound second-order Fresnel lens was removed in 1994. It was the last lens floating on a mercury bath in use in New England. Local residents lobbied for the preservation and display of the lens, which is now on display at Cape Elizabeth Town Hall.

The 1878 keeper's house next to the east tower is now privately owned. The house, after major additions in the late 1990s, is vastly changed from the way it looked when Edward Hopper painted it.

The east light at Cape Elizabeth, one of the most handsome cast-iron lighthouses of its era, remains an active aid to navigation with a modern VRB-25 rotating optic producing a sequence of four white flashes every 15 seconds. The optic and related equipment are still maintained by the Coast Guard.

In May 2000, the east tower was licensed by the Coast Guard to the American Lighthouse Foundation (ALF). The tower's foundation was repaired in the fall of 2008.

The organization is raising funds for additional restoration; for more information, contact the American Lighthouse Foundation, P.O. Box 565, Rockland, ME 04841; (207) 594-4174; www.lighthousefoundation.org.

The grounds immediately around the lighthouse are not open to the public. Views are available at the end of Two Lights Road; turn at the "Two Lights State Park" sign on Route 77 and follow the signs to the lighthouses.

CHAPTER 7

Portland Head Light in October 2007. *Photo by the author.*

Portland Head Light

1791

Edward Rowe Snow, the popular historian and raconteur of the New England coast, wrote in his book *Famous New England Lighthouses,* "Portland Head and its light seem to symbolize the state of Maine— rocky coast, breaking waves, sparkling water and clear, pure salt air." The hundreds of thousands of people who visit Portland Head each year would agree; this is one of the most strikingly beautiful lighthouse locations in New England.

The city of Portland took its name from the headland where the lighthouse now stands, but Portland Head is actually within the present boundaries of the town of Cape Elizabeth. Portland, which was known as Falmouth until 1786, was America's sixth busiest port by the 1790s. There were no lighthouses on the coast of Maine when 74 merchants petitioned the Massachusetts government (Maine was part of Massachusetts at the time) in 1784 for a light at Portland Head, on the northeast coast of Cape Elizabeth, to mark the entrance to Portland Harbor.

In 1785, Joseph Noyes, representing the General Court of Massachusetts, was directed to look into the construction of a lighthouse at "Portland Point." The deaths of two people in a 1787 shipwreck at Bangs (now Cushing) Island, near Portland Head, led to the appropriation of $750 for a lighthouse, and construction began. The project was slowed by insufficient funds, although Governor John Hancock requested money for the building of "a small building for the keeper" in February 1790.

Construction didn't progress until the federal government assumed management of the nation's lighthouses. In August 1790, Congress appropriated an additional $1,500 for the completion of the station. President George Washington remarked that it should be possible to build the tower from rubblestone found in the fields and shores of Cape Elizabeth, and that the stone could be "handled nicely when hauled by oxen on a drag."

Two local masons, Jonathan Bryant and John Nichols, built the rubblestone lighthouse. Bryant owned a limekiln operation at the foot of India Street in Portland. The original plan was for a 58-foot tower, but when it was realized that the light would be blocked from the south by a headland, the local lighthouse superintendent, Gen. Benjamin Lincoln, decided that the tower should be 72 feet high to the base of the lantern. Bryant resigned over the change, and Nichols finished the lighthouse and a small dwelling in late 1790.

President Washington approved the appointment of Capt. Joseph Greenleaf, a veteran of the American Revolution, as first keeper. The light went into service on January 10, 1791, with whale oil lamps showing a fixed white light. At first, Greenleaf received no salary as keeper; his payment was the right to fish and farm and live in the keeper's house. As early as November 1791, Greenleaf wrote that he couldn't afford to remain keeper without financial compensation. In a June 1792 letter, he complained of many hardships. During the previous winter, he wrote, the ice on the lantern glass was often so thick that he had to melt it off. In 1793, Greenleaf was granted an annual salary of $160.

Greenleaf died of an apparent stroke while in his boat on the Fore River in October 1795. According to the *Eastern Argus,* he had "faithfully discharged his duty to the satisfaction of those who occupy their business on great waters."

After a short stay by David Duncan, Barzillai Delano, a blacksmith who had lobbied for the appointment when the lighthouse was first built, became keeper in 1796. Delano's salary of $225 yearly was raised to $300 in 1812, after a petition with 22 signatures was submitted in his behalf.

In 1809, Delano wrote the local superintendent, complaining of leaks in the tower. Wooden sheathing was suggested as a remedy, but the plan was never carried out. By 1810, the woodwork in the lighthouse and keeper's house was damp and rotting. Part of the problem was that the keeper was storing a year's supply of oil in one room, which put great stress on the floor. Repairs were made, and an oil shed was added.

The tower continued to have problems with leaks. In November 1812, the contractor Winslow Lewis offered the opinion that the upper 20 feet of the tower was very poorly built. The lantern, which was only 5 feet in diameter, was also badly constructed.

Lewis recommended reducing the tower's height by 20 feet and adding a new lantern. Lewis carried out these changes in 1813, along with the installation of a system of lamps and reflectors designed by Lewis himself, at a cost of $2,100. About 25 feet of stonework at the top of the tower was removed. Apparently, the headland that blocked the light to the south was no longer of great concern.

The contractor Henry Dyer of Cape Elizabeth built a new keeper's house in 1816 for $1,175. The one-story stone cottage was 20 by 34 feet and comprised two rooms, an attached kitchen, and an attic. The kitchen ell was attached to outbuildings, which, in turn, were joined to the tower. The joining of the house to the tower had been requested in 1809 by Delano, who complained that the space between the buildings was often frozen over in winter and that the sea sometimes washed over the area.

Barzillai Delano died in 1820; his son, James, later served as keeper from 1854 to 1861. Joshua Freeman, who would become known for his jovial hospitality, became keeper in 1820. Freeman kept a supply of rum and other spirits in a cupboard, and he'd sell drinks for three cents a glass to visitors who came to fish. The top-shelf liquor was reserved for the local minister.

An 1825 article in the *Eastern Argus* described the pleasures of a visit to Portland Head:

> *I know of no excursion as pleasant as a jaunt to the Light House. There our friend Freeman is always at home, and ready to serve you. There you can angle in safety and comfort for the cunning cunner, while old ocean is rolling majestically at your feet, and when wearied and fatigued with this amusement, you will find a pleasant relaxation in tumbling the huge rocks from the brinks of the steep and rocky precipices. . . . I know of no equal to a ride or sail to the Light House and earnestly recommend it to all poor devils who, like myself, are afflicted with the dyspepsia, gout, or any of the diseases to which human flesh is heir.*

Richard Lee succeeded Freeman as keeper in April 1840 at a yearly salary of $350. Lee was in charge when the civil engineer I. W. P. Lewis (Winslow Lewis's nephew) visited in August 1842 for his important report to Congress. Lewis found the tower in bad condition, its mortar inferior, woodwork rotten, and roof leaky. The 15 lamps and corresponding reflectors were out of alignment, and four of them faced the land "to no purpose." The dwelling's walls were cracked in several places and leaky. Lewis recommended fewer lamps, more properly aligned. He concluded that the station's condition was "far inferior to what such a locality requires." In a statement included in Lewis's report, Lee added that he was allowed no boat and that he had to pay for the use of adjacent land for pasturage, since the government land provided "barely room for a garden."

A new system of 13 lamps and reflectors was installed, along with a new lantern, in 1850. In August of that year, an inspection found that the bad mortar in the tower allowed rain to pass through, and that the dwelling was also "very leaky." An examination by the newly commissioned U.S. Lighthouse Board in 1851 revealed that the new reflectors were already badly scratched. The oil was of poor quality, the house was leaky and cracking, and rats were undermining the tower. The keeper, John F. Watts, was poorly trained and had received no written instructions on the operation of the light. He was forced to hire a man to instruct him for two days.

Improvements were made in the following years, after the establishment of the new, efficient Lighthouse Board. A fourth-order Fresnel lens replaced the multiple lamps and reflectors in 1855. In the same year, a bell tower with a 1,500-pound bell was installed, the tower was lined with brick, and a cast-iron spiral stairway was added.

Following the 1864 wreck of the Liverpool vessel *Bohemian,* in which 40 immigrants died, the light was further improved. The tower was raised 20 feet with an addition constructed of brick, and a more powerful Fresnel lens was installed. The 1865 annual report of the Lighthouse Board stated, "It is believed now that the entrance to this harbor is so completely lighted that navigation in and out is attended with little or no danger."

Joshua Freeman Strout, who was born in 1827, became keeper in 1869 at a salary of $620 per year. Strout's mother had worked as a housekeeper at Portland Head for Joshua Freeman in the 1820s, and

One of the earliest photos of Portland Head Light Station, before the tower was raised by 20 feet in 1864. The bell tower at the right was installed in 1855. *National Archives.*

Joshua Freeman Strout was the principal keeper at Portland Head Light 1869–1904. *Courtesy of the American Lighthouse Foundation.*

she named her son for the keeper. Joshua Strout went to sea at the age of 11 and served as the cook on a tugboat by the time he was 18. He later captained a number of vessels and traveled as far as Cuba and South America. Injuries suffered in a severe fall from the masthead of the *Andres* forced him to give up his life at sea in exchange for the somewhat more tranquil life of a lighthouse keeper.

Strout's wife, Mary (Berry), was named an assistant keeper at a salary of $480 per year. She held the position until 1877, when her son Joseph took on the title of assistant keeper. Joshua and Mary Strout raised 11 children at the station. Three of their sons—Charles, Stephen, and John—were all lost at sea during the family's years at Portland Head.

Lighthouse life wasn't always tranquil. A hurricane on September 8, 1869, knocked the fog bell from its perch, nearly killing Joshua Strout. A tower with a new bell and a Stevens striking mechanism was installed the following year. The bell was replaced in 1872 by a fog trumpet formerly used on Monhegan Island, but the bell remained in place as an auxiliary signal.

The poet Henry Wadsworth Longfellow, who was born in Portland in 1807, was a frequent visitor in his younger years. Longfellow's 1849 poem "The Lighthouse" was undoubtedly inspired by his many hours at Portland Head. Here's the first verse of the poem:

> *The rocky ledge runs far out into the sea*
> *And on its outer point, some miles away,*
> *The lighthouse lifts its massive masonry,*
> *A pillar of fire by night, of cloud by day.*

Later in his life, Longfellow would walk to the lighthouse from the city and visit with Joshua Strout. A favorite lounging place of the poet was a white rock on the south side of the tower. The rock is now marked with a sign bearing lines from "The Lighthouse."

Portland Head was always a tourist attraction, and a favorite pastime of visitors was watching the crashing surf during storms. A tremendous storm swept the Maine coast in November 1871, doing great damage to Portland's wharves. The *Eastern Argus* reported that many people went to Portland Head to view the spectacular surf, and Joshua Strout "kindly furnished every reasonable facility for the accommodation of the sight seekers." The sound of the waves striking the shore was described as "a roar like the voice of many Niagaras."

In his 1876 book, *Portland and Vicinity,* Edward H. Elwell reported that a few years earlier a party had gone to Portland Head to watch the waves during a gale—possibly the storm of November 1871. Two carriage drivers who had taken the group out ventured too far onto the rocks and were swept away. Their bodies were recovered several days later.

Upon the completion of Halfway Rock Light offshore in Casco Bay in 1871, the Lighthouse Board felt that Portland Head Light had lost its value as a major seacoast light, as it served local maritime interests exclusively. The 1864 brick addition was reported to be dilapidated, and the lantern was in poor condition. For these reasons the tower was shortened by 20 feet in 1883, and a new lantern and a fourth-order lens were installed. At the same time, the fuel for the light was changed from lard oil to kerosene.

Joseph Woodbury Strout was the principal keeper at Portland Head 1904–28. *Courtesy of the Thomas Memorial Library in Cape Elizabeth.*

Less than two years after it was shortened, the tower was again raised 20 feet and a second-order lens was installed. The improved fixed white light went into service on January 15, 1885.

On Christmas Eve in 1886, the British bark *Annie C. Maguire* ran ashore on the rocks at Portland Head during a blinding snowstorm described by Joseph Strout as so bad that "even Santa Claus was afraid to be out." The *Maguire* began its life in 1853 as a New York–built clipper called the *Golden State;* it was sold and had its rigging and name changed in 1883. The *Maguire,* captained by

Daniel O'Neil (spelled O'Niel in some accounts), was trying to take shelter in Portland Harbor in the storm when it smashed into a ledge a stone's throw from the lighthouse. Keeper Joshua Strout heard the shouts of the crew over the sound of the surf, and he informed his son Joseph, "There's a ship in the backyard."

The Strouts took quick action, grabbing a ladder from storage and climbing down onto the rocks. They laid the ladder across the rocks to the ship so that it became a makeshift gangway. Mary Strout shed light on the scene by burning blankets that had been cut into strips and soaked in kerosene. In addition to the captain and 15 crewmen, the passengers included the captain's wife and 12-year-old son. All aboard made it safely across the ladder to solid ground.

In a 1929 interview, Joseph Strout recalled what happened next: "The day before we had killed eight chickens so that we could have a great feed on Christmas. Ma made all eight into the best pie you ever tasted. . . . There was nothing on that boat to eat. All they had was a large supply of salt beef and macaroni, with lime juice to keep from getting scurvy. For months that crew had not tasted real food. Once they got that chicken pie into them, the whole gang wanted to stay."

An examination of the vessel on Christmas Day revealed that the rocks had torn into its hull and the ship had flooded. Everything that could be moved was taken off the bark, and a junk dealer purchased the remnants a few days later. Some fittings were salvaged, and the

The wreck of the British bark *Annie C. Maguire* on December 24, 1886. *From the collection of the author.*

remains of the *Maguire* were broken apart by another storm early on New Year's Day.

It later became a tradition for keepers to paint a large rock facing the lighthouse with an inscription memorializing the wreck. The inscription can still be seen: "Annie C. Maguire, shipwrecked here, Christmas Eve 1886."

The Strouts performed another dramatic rescue during a storm on November 30, 1887, when the schooner *D. W. Hammond* was driven onto the rocks north of the station. Joseph Strout and his brother Gil, who was also an assistant keeper, pulled the nearly frozen captain and two crewmen from the vessel and rushed them inside the keeper's house, where they were revived through the efforts of Mary Strout and her daughter-in-law.

Just a month later, on December 28, Portland was pelted by a storm that brought heavy rain and winds of 50 miles per hour. The gale was nothing extraordinary until, about 9:30 p.m., the Strouts watched in horror as they saw a "great wave," in the shape of a pyramid, approaching the light station through the rain. A farmer about two miles away was quoted in newspapers: "When the wave was coming it made a fearful roar, but when it struck the cliffs, it seemed as though it fairly smashed them to pieces."

The wave struck the outer line of rocks, cleared the top of the lighthouse, and smashed into the fog signal building. "Great iron stays were snapped as though they had been pipe stems," according to newspaper accounts. When the wave receded, it took everything that wasn't secured back to sea with it, including boulders weighing tons.

In August 1887, an engine for the fog signal was moved from Boston Light to Portland Head to replace an engine that had worn out. By 1888, a new brick fog signal building, slightly more than 20 by 20 feet in size, was erected to replace the one that had been badly damaged by the great wave of December 1887.

The old stone dwelling was removed in 1891 to make room for a new wood-frame double dwelling, 42½ feet by 42 feet at its foundation. Along with the new house, a small brick oil house was added to store the station's kerosene. The old house was reportedly moved to become a private home nearby.

The light was extinguished from April to July 1898 during the Spanish-American War, out of fear that it would help enemy vessels. Fort Williams, established adjacent to the light station in 1872, was enlarged around this time. The lighthouse lens was padded so the firing of the fort's guns wouldn't injure it.

Early-1900s postcard view of Portland Head. *From the collection of the author.*

Anyone passing through the grounds during this period had to explain his presence to a sentry. Once, when he was returning to the lighthouse, Joshua Strout was stopped by the sentry, who didn't recognize the old man. "Where do you want to go?" he asked. Strout replied, "Well, I was thinking of going down to the light." When asked if he knew someone there, the keeper responded, "I guess maybe I know the lighthouse keeper. I've brought up his family there for about 35 years."

The year 1900 saw a major repointing of the tower; many of the original stones were replaced. In the same year, two new oil engines with air compressors replaced the old fog signal equipment. Five hundred feet of piping installed around the same time connected the station to the public water supply.

In an 1898 interview, Joshua Strout said that he had gone as long as 17 years in a stretch without taking time off, and as long as two years without going as far as Portland. Strout, the oldest keeper on the Maine coast at the time, retired in 1904. He died three years later, at 81. His son Joseph Woodbury Strout, who was described as short and stout but rugged, became the next keeper.

Joseph Strout remained at the station until 1928, ending 59 years of the family at Portland Head. In 1910, he was quoted in the *Lewiston Journal:*

> *We've all got the lighthouse fever in our blood. . . . Father was keeper before me. Joshua Freeman Strout, that was his name, and*

a fine old man he was too. He was named for Captain Joshua Freeman. He kept the light, too, Captain Freeman did, in the days when they burned whale oil and had sixteen lamps. When grandmother was a girl of sixteen, she worked at Cap'n Freeman's and after she married and father was born, she named him Joshua Freeman Strout. Old Cap'n Freeman used to sit in a big armchair with a coil of rope near him so if a shipwreck came sudden he would be prepared.

An African parrot named Billy was a well-known member of the Strout household for many years beginning in 1887. When bad weather approached, Billy would tell the keeper, "Joe, let's start the horn. It's foggy!" Billy became an avid fan of radio in his declining years and lived to be over 80.

In his book *Lighthouses of the Maine Coast and the Men Who Keep Them*, Robert Thayer Sterling called Joseph Strout "one of the most popular lightkeepers of his day or any yet to come. His genial disposition, his hearty laugh, together with his good stories of the sea, won him the admiration of all who met him." Sterling, who served as an assistant keeper under Joseph Strout, added that when Strout retired in 1928, "the summer guests lost a very beloved man."

Joseph Strout's son, John A. Strout, born in 1891, continued the family tradition by serving as an assistant keeper. It was John Strout who first painted the words memorializing the *Annie Maguire* wreck on a rock near the lighthouse, on the day he assumed his duties as assistant keeper in January 1912. He had to chip away some of the rock to make a flat surface before he could paint.

John A. Strout's son, John, wrote in *Lighthouse Digest* that his father recalled, as a boy of seven, hearing the whistle salute of the steamer *Portland* as it passed. The *Portland* sank in a tremendous snowstorm in November 1898, and around 200 lives were lost. At Portland Head, the foghorn sounded for 72 straight hours during the storm.

For a time, the buildings at the light station received serious damage from practice gunfire from neighboring Fort Williams. The U.S. Lighthouse Service Bulletin of September 1, 1916, related that "windows were forced out, finish ripped off, roof torn open," and it also reported "injury to the brickwork of the three chimneys of the double dwelling." On one occasion, two of the chimneys were completely severed at the bottom. Casings were subsequently installed to protect the chimneys.

John W. Cameron, a native of Southport, Maine, was an assistant keeper at Portland Head beginning 1904, after time at the nearby light

John W. Cameron was an assistant keeper at Portland Head 1904–28 and principal keeper 1928–29. *Courtesy of the U.S. Lighthouse Society.*

stations at Spring Point Ledge and Cape Elizabeth (Two Lights). Cameron took over as principal keeper when Joseph Strout retired in 1928. The light was converted from kerosene to electricity the following year, and Cameron later commented that the change was a welcome one, as it "relieved the keepers of the chore of 'lighting up' each night." The characteristic of the light was changed at this time from fixed to a sequence of two seconds on, two seconds off.

Cameron's tenure as principal keeper was brief, as he reached the mandatory retirement age of 70 in 1929. When Cameron retired, Frank O. Hilt became principal keeper. Hilt, who was originally from St. George, Maine, went to sea at a young age and eventually became the captain of the schooner *Mary Langdon* and other vessels. Beginning in 1913, he served as an assistant keeper and then principal keeper at the isolated light station at Matinicus Rock.

Hilt remained in charge at Portland Head until 1944. One of his more unusual accomplishments was the construction of a giant checkerboard near the base of the lighthouse tower. Edward Rowe Snow, in his book *The Romance of Casco Bay,* wrote that one of his most delightful memories of Portland Head was photographing Hilt contemplating a move on the giant board during a checkers match with Snow's wife, Anna-Myrle. Hilt "in his prime was a 300-pound giant," according to Snow.

The station got a new fog signal in 1938, when a three-horn diaphragm chime horn system replaced the old Daboll trumpet. The new signal included a large horn pointing toward Halfway Rock, and two smaller horns facing Portland Harbor and the Portland Lightship.

The last civilian keeper before the Coast Guard took over was Robert Thayer Sterling, a journalist who wrote the book *Lighthouses of the Maine Coast and the Men Who Keep Them* in 1935. Sterling, who was from Peaks Island in Portland, Maine, entered the Lighthouse

Robert T. Sterling, left, and Frank O. Hilt. Sterling was an assistant keeper at Portland Head 1928–44, then principal keeper 1944–46. Hilt was the principal keeper 1929–44. *Courtesy of the Maine Lighthouse Museum.*

Service in 1915 and spent time at Ram Island Ledge, Great Duck Island, Seguin Island, and Cape Elizabeth (Two Lights) before arriving at Portland Head as an assistant in 1928. He succeeded Hilt as principal keeper in 1944.

An interesting story of the Sterling years at Portland Head concerns the keeper's dog, Chang. Sterling's wife, Martha, liked to do her knitting in a favorite chair, near a window. On one particular evening, Chang was growling at the chair with such intensity that Martha decided to do her knitting in another part of the house. Just after she left, a huge wave hit the house, breaking the window and sending shards of glass all over the chair.

Sterling, who retired in 1946, declared Portland Head the most desirable of all light stations for keepers. On the first day of his retirement, Sterling fell in his yard and broke a rib. As a result, he had to put his plans to attend some Boston Red Sox games on hold.

The light was dark for three years during World War II, from June 1942 to June 1945. The station was also off-limits to unauthorized visitors for much of the war.

After the war, a constant stream of tourists was once again a way of life at Portland Head. Under the station's first Coast Guard keeper, William Lockhart, the station was open to the public Monday through

Friday from 10:00 a.m. to 3:00 p.m., except when the fog signal was sounding. Lockhart said that most visitors were more interested in enjoying the views than they were in the lighthouse's history. Most were thrilled with the scenery, but one woman from the Midwest expressed disappointment when she saw the Atlantic Ocean for the first time. "I thought it was bigger," she told the Coast Guard crew.

There was little privacy for keepers and their families. When Earle Benson was keeper in the 1950s, a woman once walked right into the keeper's house and sat at the kitchen table. She insisted that Benson and his wife were government employees, and she demanded service.

Wes Gamage, a Coast Guard keeper in the early 1960s, was always sure to keep the doors and first-floor windows locked so tourists couldn't wander in. Once, Gamage's wife was taking a bath upstairs when several camera-toting tourists suddenly burst right into the bathroom. It turned out she had forgotten to lock one of the doors.

Severe weather has continued to plague the station in recent decades. In February 1972, Coast Guardsman Robert Allen reported to the *Maine Sunday Telegram* that a storm had torn the fog bell from its house, ripped 80 feet of steel fence out of concrete, and left the house a "foot deep in mud and flotsam, including starfish." A wave had broken a window in the house, 25 feet above the ground.

The Coast Guard keepers and their families were evacuated during a storm in March 1977. The power lines were downed and the generator burned out, leaving the lighthouse dark for the first time since World War II.

On August 7, 1989, a celebration was held at Portland Head Light commemorating the 200th anniversary of the creation of a federal lighthouse service. The day also marked the automation of Portland Head Light and the transfer of the last two Coast Guard keepers, Davis Simpson and Nathan Wasserstrom, as well as the leasing of the light station property (except the tower) to the Town of Cape Elizabeth.

Maine's Senator George Mitchell, Congressman Joseph Brennan, and the lighthouse historian F. Ross Holland spoke at the celebration while the Nantucket Lightship paraded offshore with a flotilla of Coast Guard vessels. Rear Adm. Richard Rybacki, the Coast Guard's First District commander, said in his address to the crowd: "I can think of nothing more noble. The lighthouse symbolizes all that is good in mankind. We are not here to celebrate an ending. We are here to immortalize a tradition."

The Museum at Portland Head Light opened in the former keeper's house in 1992. The museum focuses on the history of the lighthouse and nearby Fort Williams. Among the displays are the station's old seven-foot-tall second-order lens and a fifth-order lens from Squirrel Point. A garage was converted into a gift shop that now does about $500,000 worth of business yearly. Cheryl Parker was the director of the museum for its first decade of existence; the current director is a Cape Elizabeth resident, Jeanne Gross.

In October 1993, the light station property was deeded to the Town of Cape Elizabeth. For a few years, part of the keeper's house was rented as an apartment. The first tenants were two Coast Guard ensigns, Matt Stuck and Sam Eisenbeiser. Stuck declared, "There's no other place on this planet with views out of every window." There was a downside, however. One of the ensigns told reporters, "The disadvantage of living at Portland Head Light is that you're part of the scenery," referring to the constant flow of tourists.

Ed Ellis and his wife, Elaine Amass, lived in the apartment for two years. "The view is worth the visitors and the foghorn. If it wasn't, we would have left the first year," said Ellis. The former apartment is now used for offices and storage for the museum and gift shop.

It often seems that lighthouses and ghost stories go together. This one, for an old station, has few such tales. But Ellis and Amass reported that their motion-sensor alarm on the stairs sometimes went off at night when nobody—at least, nobody they could see—was there. And Geraldine Reed, who lived in the keeper's house with her husband, Coast Guardsman Tom Reed, in the 1960s, wrote in *Lighthouse Digest* that she believed there was a ghost in residence. The only place

The Nantucket Lightship anchored offshore during the August 7, 1989, celebration at Portland Head. *Photo by the author.*

she felt the presence of the ghost was in the basement of the keeper's house. "My feeling is that he was a friendly ghost and just needed to be told that his keeper days were over and he could rest in peace," she wrote.

Rainbow Construction replaced the deteriorating roof of the keeper's house in 2002, using durable modern red shingles that appear historically authentic. A $260,000 renovation of the lighthouse was completed in the spring of 2005. Some repointing was done on the 80-foot tower, and it was repainted. The keeper's house and gift shop were also painted, and some of the lighthouse's windows were replaced. Another ongoing project will extend the path around the cliff near the lighthouse and improve the site's landscaping.

The second-order Fresnel lens was replaced by a rotating DCB-36 aerobeacon in 1958. The lighthouse, now with a rotating DCB-224 exhibiting a white flash every four seconds, 101 feet above mean high water, remains an active aid to navigation, as does the automated fog signal.

The Museum at Portland Head Light has welcomed visitors from every state in the United States and over 75 countries. The museum is open June through October. There is ample parking and plenty of room for picnicking or strolling. Maine's oldest lighthouse is easily accessible by land; some tour boats out of Portland approach the lighthouse by sea. The lighthouse is located within Fort Williams Park.

A variety of cruises leaving from Portland provide views from the water. Lucky Catch Lobstering provides lighthouse photo opportunities while guiding you through the daily routines of Maine lobstermen; call (207) 233-2026 or visit www.luckycatch.com. Portland Discovery offers trips on land and sea; visit www.portlanddiscovery.com or call (207) 774-0808.

For more information on the lighthouse and museum, contact the Museum at Portland Head Light, 1000 Shore Road, Cape Elizabeth, ME 04107; (207) 799-2661; www.portlandheadlight.com.

CHAPTER 8

Ram Island Ledge Light in February 2006. *Photo by the author.*

Ram Island Ledge Light

1905

Ram Island, on the easterly approach to Portland Harbor and about a mile northeast of Portland Head, is surrounded by dangerous ledges. As early as 1855, an iron spindle was erected as a navigational aid on Ram Island Ledge, which extends to the south of Ram Island. The spindle was carried away by ice in 1868, but it was soon replaced. By 1903, the beacon on the ledge was described as a red wooden tripod, 50 feet high.

These markers were helpful in clear weather during the day, but in bad weather they were virtually invisible. Shipwrecks occurred with frequency; local tradition held that the ledge, aptly described as a "jagged disarray of hungry monsters" by the historian Herbert Milton Sylvester, claimed a vessel every seven years.

On May 27, 1866, alone, there were four wrecks. Many fishing boats and schooners struck the ledges over the years, often while trying to make Portland Harbor in bad weather. On February 24, 1900, the 400-foot trans-Atlantic Allan Line steamer *Californian,* bound for England from Portland with a crew of 96 and 21 passengers, went aground at the outer end of the ledge in a snowstorm. There was no loss of life, and the steamer was refloated six weeks later.

This near-tragedy finally convinced the federal government that a lighthouse was called for. In June 1902, Congress appropriated $83,000 for the building of a lighthouse on the ledge. An additional appropriation of $50,000 was made in March 1903.

The shipwrecks continued. The Nova Scotian schooner *Glenrosa,* carrying a cargo of coal, struck the ledge on September 20, 1902, and was a total loss, but its crew of eight survived. Then, on December 8, the fishing vessel *Cora and Lillian* ran into the east side of the ledge with a full cargo of fish. The crew managed to get safely ashore at Portland Head. The *Cora and Lillian* remained on the ledge for some time, until a severe storm swept it away.

In 1903, the federal government purchased the ledge from two Cape Elizabeth families for $500. Ram Island Ledge was submerged much of the time, and construction could take place only at low tide. Work began on May 1, 1903, with a crew of 40 men working under

James Howard of Portland. Alfred Hamilton of nearby Chebeague Island was the foreman at the ledge.

By June 30, the ledge was leveled and construction of the tower's foundation began. A 100-foot timber bulkhead was bolted to the ledge to provide protection for the workers and materials. A platform for materials, a hoisting engine, and a derrick were built on the ledge, and temporary quarters were set up for the workers on Ram Island, about 600 yards from the work site. A small steamer provided transportation between the ledge and Portland.

The Bodwell Granite Company provided granite blocks from a Vinalhaven quarry at a cost of $33,679.40. The giant blocks were prepared at Vinalhaven, shipped to Central Wharf in Portland, numbered to indicate their position, and then ferried to the ledge—which had been leveled to three feet above mean low water—aboard two sloops.

The stones near the base weighed four tons each, and the upper stones weighed about three tons each. The stones on the lowest course were secured with four iron bolts each, extending three feet into the ledge and eight feet into the blocks. The final tally of granite blocks used was 699, in 35 courses.

The first stones were laid in July 1903. Two months later, the *Kennebec Journal* reported that the lighthouse was "assuming definite shape, and climbing skyward at an astonishing rate of speed, consider-

A scene from the construction of Ram Island Ledge Light. *From the collection of the author.*

ing the nature of the work, and extremely rough and dangerous spot where it is located."

By the end of September 1903, the tower reached a height of 16 courses and 32 feet. Another congressional appropriation of $33,000 was needed to complete the project, which cost $166,000 in all. The final appropriation was made in April 1904.

A crew of 25 men worked from April to July 1904 to complete the tower, which is 70 feet tall to the base of the lantern deck. The diameter is 28 feet at the base, 24 feet at the top. Entry to the tower was achieved by climbing a ladder to the first level, below which was a 22-foot-deep cistern, lined with concrete. The next level was the galley, followed by three more levels with space for equipment and living quarters for the keepers.

The interior ironwork and exterior ladder were manufactured at the Lighthouse Service machine shop in Boston, and the interior woodwork was prepared at a storehouse in Portland. The interior walls were lined with enameled bricks.

A 26,000-pound lantern, manufactured in Atlanta, was placed on the tower and fitted with a third-order Fresnel lens from Paris. O. C. Luther, a mechanic for the Lighthouse Service, supervised this stage of the project. Including the lantern, the lighthouse reached a height of 90 feet, and the light was 77 feet above mean high water. The tower is a slightly shorter sibling of Graves Light in outer Boston Harbor, which was built almost at the same time.

In the predawn hours of January 12, 1905, just a few months before the light went into service, the *Leona,* heading from Rockland, Maine, to Rockport, Massachusetts, with a cargo of lime, struck a ledge near Ram Island as the captain tried to make Portland Harbor in a snowstorm. The captain and four crewmen launched a lifeboat and managed to stay afloat for a few hours, until the construction workers at the ledge saw one of their flares. The workers directed the lifeboat to a cove near the lighthouse and then helped the nearly frozen men get safely ashore.

The kerosene lamp was first lighted on April 10, 1905, with two white flashes every six seconds. On the night of its first lighting, Captain Dyer at the Cape Elizabeth Lifesaving Station reported that the light was "strong and brilliant." The light's flashing characteristic was produced by a clockwork mechanism that rotated the lens, which floated on a bed of mercury. The mechanism had to be wound every hour and a half by the keepers.

Work continued after the light went into operation. An iron pier was added to the ledge, extending to the west; at its end was a fog bell tower. The bell went into operation on August 28, 1905, its automatic striking machinery producing a blow every 10 seconds.

The first principal keeper was William C. Tapley, formerly at Saddleback Ledge Light and Deer Island Thorofare Light. Tapley served until 1929. There were three keepers assigned to the station; each keeper stayed for two weeks, working daily 12-hour shifts, followed by a week of shore leave.

One of the assistants for a period around 1915 was Robert Thayer Sterling, a native of Portland. Sterling later served many years at Portland Head Light and wrote the book *Lighthouses of the Maine Coast and the Men Who Keep Them* in 1935.

According to Peter Dow Bachelder, in his book *Lighthouses of Casco Bay*, Ram Island Ledge became a popular destination for adventurous tourists during the summer. Picnickers, curiosity seekers, and fishing parties were not uncommon. One enterprising visitor bragged to William Tapley that he earned $500 a summer by gathering the sea moss that was plentiful on the rocks.

Joe Johansen was an assistant keeper for the Coast Guard in 1949–50. He later told an interviewer about his life at Ram Island Ledge:

> *You could have been living in the 1800s because, other than the link with the radio, there were no conveniences at all. Nothing.*
>
> *You went up a ladder onto a pier where there was a 15-foot pea-pod hanging on davits. That was your access for going shopping over to Cushing or Peaks Island around two miles away. When I was first on Ram, we rowed there and back.*
>
> *It was lonesome in a way, but you were never really lonely, because there were always two of you aboard. In the winters the nights were kind of long because you split the watch. . . . You usually stood watch in the galley because that's where your only source of heat was: a kerosene stove, which we used for cooking and heat.*

The lens still turned on a mercury bath and the rotating mechanism had to be manually wound every 90 minutes during Johansen's stay. Occasionally, the man on watch might fall asleep and miss a winding. "That was really a ding on your record," said Johansen.

There was no plumbing in the tower. The keepers kept a "slop bucket" under the sink, which had to be carefully dumped overboard periodically. A privy was located on the pier—"just a two-holer," according to Johansen. A visit to the privy could be frightening in times of storms and high seas. "You'd sit your stern on there," said Johansen, "and, boy, sometimes you'd get chased off pretty good!"

U.S. Coast Guard aerial view of Ram Island Ledge Light.

Johansen once spent 45 days straight at the light during rough winter weather. As their food supply ran low, he and another keeper were reduced to eating oatmeal three times a day.

The light was electrified in 1958 by means of an underwater cable extending from Portland Head. The light and fog signal were monitored remotely by the keepers at Portland Head Light Station, which enabled the Coast Guard to remove the keepers from Ram Island Ledge in 1959.

The light was converted to solar power in January 2001. The solar panels mounted on the south side of the tower provide power for two large batteries supplying the light and fog signal. Today, a modern 300-millimeter optic exhibits two white flashes every 10 seconds, and an automatic foghorn blasts once every 10 seconds as needed.

In 2008, it was announced that the lighthouse would be made available to a suitable new steward under the guidelines of the National Historic Lighthouse Preservation Act of 2000. There were no applicants, so the property was sold at auction in September 2010 to Dr. Jeffrey Florman of Windham, Maine, for $190,000.

Ram Island Ledge Light can be clearly seen from Portland Head Light and from some of the tour boats leaving Portland. Portland Discovery offers trips on land and sea, and their Lighthouse Lovers Cruise passes close by Ram Island Ledge Light; visit www.portlanddiscovery.com or call (207) 774-0808.

CHAPTER 9

Spring Point Ledge Light in September 2005. *Photo by the author.*

Spring Point Ledge Light
1897

Spring Point Ledge is a dangerous obstruction on the west side of the main shipping channel from the south into Portland Harbor, just under two miles north-northwest of Portland Head. An 1896 newspaper article explained how the local fishermen found their way into the harbor while avoiding the ledge before the lighthouse was built. They would approach the tall, prominent Portland Observatory on the city's Munjoy Hill, and when it looked like Waterville Street ran right up to it, they knew they were in the right channel.

This was fine for small vessels that could skirt the ledge, but the strategy was no help to large vessels that required a wider berth. Many vessels ran aground on the ledge, including the schooner *Nancy* in 1832 and the bark *Harriet S. Jackson,* which ran up on the ledge during a severe storm in March 1876. A spar buoy positioned near the ledge did little to prevent the accidents.

Requests from seven steamship companies convinced the Lighthouse Board, in 1891, to ask Congress to fund a light and fog bell at the ledge. The steamship companies had carried more than 518,000 passengers through the area during the previous year.

The Lighthouse Board, in its 1891 annual report, stated that a light and fog signal at the ledge would be "of great service to vessels making their way into Portland Harbor in thick weather." A bell buoy off Cushing Island was the only aid to vessels approaching the harbor once they had passed Portland Head, and the report pointed out that the bell buoy made no sound in calm weather. The board concluded:

> *In view of the excellence and importance of the harbor, the very large number of vessels which annually resort to it for refuge, the great number of passengers carried into it, which will doubtless steadily increase with the increasing number of people who resort to the coast of Maine in midsummer, and the frequency and density of the fogs at the very period when the passenger traffic is greatest, it is recommended that provision be made for the establishment upon Spring Point Ledge a fog bell and a light of the fifth order.*

It was recommended that a lighthouse similar to those built at Goose Rocks and Crabtree Ledge be established for $45,000.

No immediate action was taken, and in the meantime the schooner *Anna Currier,* headed for Boston with a load of lumber, ran into the ledge on August 12, 1892. The Lighthouse Board's request to Congress was repeated each year until, on March 2, 1895, a sum of $20,000 was appropriated. A second appropriation of $25,000 was made on June 11, 1896.

The contractor who built the lighthouse, Thomas Dwyer, was also responsible for some prominent buildings in New York City, including a wing of the Metropolitan Museum and several buildings at City College.

The plans originally called for the station to go into service by the end of 1896. Work on the foundation began in August, but a storm in September did considerable damage to the iron caisson plates that had been put into place. There was a delay obtaining more of the iron plates from Pennsylvania. The crew worked long hours when work resumed, but an inspection charged that the wrong kind of cement was being used, and the project was again delayed. The matter was eventually resolved, but work progressed slowly through the winter. The light and fog bell finally went into service on May 24, 1897. The first keeper was William A. Lane.

The fifth-order Fresnel lens exhibited a flash every five seconds, 54 feet above mean high water. The light was red except for a white sector that indicated the safe channel into Portland Harbor. A fog bell, hung on the side of the tower, sounded a double blow every 12 seconds by means of a striking mechanism that used 800 pounds of weights.

The lighthouse is a fairly typical "sparkplug-style" tower of the period, built on a cylindrical, cast-iron caisson, 25 feet in diameter, filled with concrete. Unlike many of this type, however, the super-structure is built of brick rather than cast iron. The caisson was painted black, and the tower was originally painted red. In November 1897, the color of the tower was changed to white.

The lighthouse had a storeroom and cistern in the basement, inside the upper part of the caisson. The next level served as the galley. Two levels of living quarters, a watch room, and the lantern topped that. An oil room in the basement contained a 239-gallon tank for the kerosene that fueled the light until it was converted to electric operation in 1934.

This was a stag station: a male keeper and assistant keeper lived inside the tower. Keepers had to be creative in getting their exercise. Somebody figured that it took 56 jogs around the tower's main deck to make one mile. Once, a keeper was running laps in this fashion and forgot to close a trap door. He slipped through the opening and only a ladder prevented him from falling 17 feet to the rock ledge and swirling waves.

In its early years, the lighthouse's foundation was battered and damaged by ice. Granite blocks were piled around the foundation to protect it, and there have been no further problems.

Daniel J. Doyle was an assistant keeper from 1915 to 1918. He occupied his spare time by playing cribbage and building ship models. Doyle had a family living in Portland. His schedule called for him to go ashore after two weeks at the lighthouse, but stormy weather sometimes prevented him from leaving the station for up to two months at a stretch. In 1999, Doyle's daughter, Barbara Ward, told the *Portland Press Herald,* "It was a rough life. It was confining . . . and you had to be really alert and pay attention to what you were doing." Just the same, she says, "He enjoyed every minute of it." Doyle left his lighthouse job, which paid $516 per year, for a better-paying job with the fire department.

One of the light's best-known keepers was Aaron Augustus "Gus" Wilson, a native of Bass Harbor, Maine. He earned a living as a fisherman and boatbuilder before joining the Lighthouse Service at the age of 50. After time at Goose Rocks and Cape Elizabeth lights, he came to Spring Point Ledge Light in 1917 as an assistant. He succeeded his own brother as principal keeper in 1931 and remained in charge until 1934.

In July 1928, Wilson made the newspapers when he reported that he had sighted a white whale, 30 feet "from stem to stern," from the lighthouse. "I have heard tell of white whales," Wilson told a reporter, "but I have never seen one before. This fellow was all white without a black spot on him anywhere."

Wilson gained wide fame as one of New England's most accomplished carvers of wooden bird decoys. He carved a variety of ducks, shorebirds, seagulls, and songbirds; it's been estimated that his total production was in excess of 5,000 carvings. "Gus whittled every spare moment," said Fred

Gus Wilson, a keeper at Spring Point Ledge Light 1917–34, gained fame as an accomplished carver of wooden bird decoys. *From the collection of the author.*

Anderson, a local man who spent much time with the keeper. Wilson carved duck decoys by the hundreds and sold them to a store in Portland for 75 cents each. He was renowned for his carving skill and imagination, and his work became highly collectible. One of Wilson's decoys fetched $195,500 at a 2005 auction. His work has been displayed at the Boston Museum of Fine Arts and at the Shelburne Museum in Vermont.

A northeast storm in June 1931 caused coastal damage and swollen rivers in Maine. During the storm, the freighter *Shooters Island*, with a crew of 35, went aground at Sprint Point Ledge. There were no injuries, and the vessel was eventually pulled off the ledge by two tugboats, a Coast Guard cutter, and two lighthouse tenders.

For some years, the keepers at Spring Point Ledge also monitored nearby Portland Breakwater Light. The light was electrified in 1934. Then, in 1951, a 900-foot breakwater was constructed with 50,000 tons of granite, which joined the lighthouse to the mainland.

Under the Maine Lights Program coordinated by the Island Institute of Rockland, it was expected that Spring Point Ledge Light would be transferred from the Coast Guard to some other group. The City of South Portland applied to co-own the property with Southern Maine Technical College, but in October 1997 the city council voted to withdraw the application after much debate. A handicapped-rights activist had threatened to take the city to court if the lighthouse wasn't made handicapped-accessible, which would have cost approximately $250,000.

In March 1998, the Spring Point Museum was allowed to make a late application to the Maine Lights Selection Committee. The museum pulled together the Spring Point Ledge Light Trust, made up of local residents, businesspeople, museum members, and city representatives. The chairman of the museum's board of directors answered the handicapped-access issue by pointing out that the Army Corps of Engineers owns the breakwater, so the owner of the lighthouse is not legally responsible for access. On April 28, 1998, the Maine Lights Selection Committee announced the transfer of Spring Point Ledge Light to the Spring Point Ledge Light Trust.

On Saturday, May 22, 1999, the lighthouse was opened to the public for the first time in its history. About 500 people visited that day, braving a chilly wind that swept the breakwater.

In 2004, a six-year effort by the Spring Point Ledge Light Trust culminated in the replacement of the badly deteriorated iron canopy over the structure's lower gallery. Atlantic Mechanical of Wiscasset, Maine, completed the overhaul in July 2004. During the first stage of the

A crew from Atlantic Mechanical replaced the lower gallery roof in July 2004. *Photo by the author.*

$52,000 job, Atlantic Mechanical workers removed all 32 plates of the canopy, then cleaned and painted all the supporting rafters and fittings.

Using the originals as templates, the workers fabricated new panels made of steel and powder-coated them using a high-heat process before installation. When the lighthouse had been built in 1897, the canopy plates were installed using rivets. Since that type of construction isn't done anymore, the new panels were installed with stainless steel bolts that look much like the earlier rivets.

Spring Point Ledge Light, still an active aid to navigation, is easily reached by land, and tour boats and ferries leaving Portland pass by. The Lighthouse Lovers Cruise offered by Portland Discovery provides an excellent view; visit www.portlanddiscovery.com or call (207) 774-0808. The amphibious vehicle tours of Downeast Duck Adventures offer a view; call (207) 774- 3825 or visit www.downeastducktours.com.

There is limited free parking nearby, and the public may walk out on the breakwater to the lighthouse. Be sure to be extra careful if you walk out; the rocks are uneven with gaps between them. Volunteers of the Spring Point Ledge Light Trust open the lighthouse for frequent public tours in the summer; call or check www.springpointlight.org for the latest schedule. For more information, write to Spring Point Ledge Light Trust, P.O. Box 2311, South Portland, ME 04106; (207) 699-2676.

CHAPTER 10

Portland Breakwater Light in January 2008. *Photo by the author.*

Portland Breakwater Light

1855, 1875

This little lighthouse is a beloved South Portland landmark, and its unique design makes it a favorite of lighthouse buffs. As Earle G. Shettleworth, director of the Maine Historic Preservation Commission, has written so aptly, "Portland Breakwater Light remains one of the few intact reminders of the harbor's Golden Age of Sail. As such, it should be treasured and preserved."

A fierce storm ravaged Portland Harbor in November 1831, destroying wharves and buildings. In response, a 2,500-foot protective breakwater was planned for the south side of the harbor's entrance, beginning at Stanford Point and extending out over Stanford Ledge. A lighthouse was included in the plans for the structure.

Construction on the breakwater began in 1837, and the foundation was completed later that year. An engineer reported in November that "the portion of the breakwater already constructed has been found efficacious in keeping off the heavy swell that formerly swept over the ledge at high water, and caused much damage to the shipping in the harbor." The breakwater eventually reached 1,800 feet and was uncapped for much of its length. Vessels had to pass through a narrow channel between the breakwater's end and an obstruction known as Hog Island Ledge. With no lighthouse at its end, the breakwater became more of a navigational hindrance than a help.

In September 1853, Lieut. Thornton A. Jenkins, secretary of the Lighthouse Board, recommended a sixth-order light at the end of the breakwater. "It is absolutely necessary to make a safe entrance into the harbor," he wrote, "and to guard against striking the breakwater itself, which is nearly under water at high tide, and therefore on dark nights difficult to be seen so as to be avoided."

A number of members of Portland's Board of Trade also submitted a letter requesting a "small movable light . . . under the care of some person on shore." Joseph Farwell, the captain of the steamer *Daniel Webster*, offered the opinion that a light on the breakwater would be "of more importance than anything for the protection of life and property that can be done by government on the coast of Maine."

The Lighthouse Board asked Congress in 1853 for an appropriation of $3,500 for a lighthouse and keeper's house, or for $1,000 if it was

The first (1855) Portland Breakwater Light. *U.S. Coast Guard.*

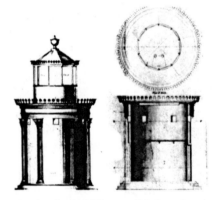

From the plans for the 1875 tower. *U.S. Coast Guard.*

deemed that no keeper's house was needed. An appropriation of $3,500 was made on August 3, 1854, but no keeper's house was built initially. Construction took about four months during the following year, and on August 1, 1855, a small, octagonal wooden tower went into service. The first keeper, W. A. Dyer, illuminated the sixth-order Fresnel lens. The fixed red light was 25 feet above mean high water.

With no keeper's house, the keeper had to walk over the breakwater to the light. This often became a battle against waves, wind, and ice. Keepers sometimes had to crawl the 1,800 feet to the lighthouse on their hands and knees.

The breakwater was extended by almost 200 feet to the northeast in the early 1870s, and the wooden lighthouse was reported to be decayed and no longer fit for service. As the work on the breakwater was in progress, the light was shown from a temporary wooden tower. After a congressional appropriation of $6,000 in June 1874, a new lighthouse was erected on a granite foundation at the end of the structure. The original tower was moved to Little Diamond Island, where it became a lookout tower at a buoy depot.

First lighted in June 1875 by Keeper Stephen Hubbard, the new Portland Breakwater Light, known locally as "Bug Light," was modeled after the Greek Choragic Monument of Lysicrates, built in Athens in

Portland Breakwater Light and keeper's house, circa early 1900s. *From the collection of the author.*

the fourth century BC. The design of the 24-foot-tall (to the tip of the lantern), cast-iron tower is unique; the cylinder, a little less than 12 feet in diameter, is surrounded by six fluted columns. It has been suggested that Thomas Ustick Walter, who designed the cast-iron dome on the U.S. Capitol, may have had something to do with designing the lighthouse.

The lighthouse held a sixth-order Fresnel lens, and the focal plane of the light was 30 feet above mean high water. The characteristic was changed from fixed to flashing red in 1879, and a clockwork mechanism was installed to rotate the lens.

The walk on the breakwater remained difficult, but still no keeper's house was built. The trip out was made somewhat easier by the addition of an iron handrail on the breakwater, 1,990 feet long, in 1886.

A tiny dwelling, a wood-frame structure with two rooms, was finally built adjacent to the lighthouse in 1889. The house presented an unusual and precarious appearance as it hung over the edge of the breakwater on both sides. Two more rooms and an attic were added in 1903.

In 1897, a 400-pound fog bell was relocated from the nearby Stanford Ledge Buoy to the breakwater, and new striking machinery was installed by 1899. A 1,000-pound bell was installed at the base of the tower in 1903. In the following year, 200 tons of riprap stones were piled around the outer end of the breakwater to afford more protection for the lighthouse.

William Tarlton Holbrook, keeper from 1910 to 1919, lived in the dwelling with his wife, Evelyn, along with their son, Elias; his wife,

Florence; and their daughter, Grace. Elias Holbrook commuted via rowboat to a job at a lobster company on Portland's Custom House Wharf.

Correspondence from February 1914 illustrates a problem of light stations with only one keeper—the keeper had to sleep sometime. A letter to William Holbrook from the district inspector indicated that a complaint had been received from the captain of the steamer *Bay State* that the station's fog bell had not been sounding at 3:44 a.m. during a recent thick fog. Holbrook replied that he had sounded the bell from 7:30 to 10:30 p.m. The weather was clear at 11:00 p.m., and he went to bed. He was awakened by a whistle blast from the *Bay State,* and he had the bell sounding again by 3:45 a.m., one minute after the time of the complaint. The inspector, showing no sympathy, wrote back, "This office regrets that such reports are received, and you are cautioned to make every effort in the future to have the fog signal at your station in operation during foggy weather."

Two more children were born to Florence and Elias Holbrook at the lighthouse: William (Bill) in 1911 and Raymond (Ray) in 1913. Many of Ray Holbrook's memories are recorded in a memoir in the collection of the South Portland Historical Society. He described the dwelling: a kitchen, a dining room, and one bedroom downstairs and two bedrooms upstairs. Outside the dining room window it was a sheer drop of around 15 feet to the water. Sometimes the window would break in storms, and the wind and rain swept inside. The only heat in the house was from a stove in the kitchen, and in the winter the boys would dress and undress next to the stove. There was no electricity and no telephone.

Next to the keeper's house were a storage shed, a cistern building, and a two-seater outhouse connected to a shaft leading to the harbor below. "A draft of wind blew up through the shaft at high tide," Raymond recalled. "We were very careful to check the wind and tide before going out there!"

Young Bill and Ray played on a wooden platform outside the dwelling. A favorite pastime was throwing things into the water and watching them float away, but that wasn't so much fun for Ray when Bill threw his prized teddy bear overboard. During World War I, Ray and Bill marched and drilled on the platform with wooden guns, drums, and flags.

The parade of passing boats and ships was always entertaining, and Capt. Jesse Brewer, the boys' uncle, would always blow his horn when he passed in his two-masted coaster, transporting lumber. Another uncle, Capt. Naham Brewer, served as captain on some of the steamships that passed by, including the *City of Bangor* and the *City of*

Rockland. During the war, William Holbrook would sometimes row his boys out to see the naval ships in the harbor, and the sailors would shout greetings and throw candy to them.

A boat named *Ben Hur* regularly delivered water to the station, and the lighthouse tender *Hibiscus* brought supplies and occasionally an inspection party. Coal, kerosene, and paint were delivered, but firewood was salvaged from the rocks or from the water.

There were always plenty of people walking to the station in good weather, and, as Ray recalled, "Many a romance blossomed from an afternoon walk to the lighthouse." Sometimes men would play poker or shoot craps on the breakwater, and Ray and Bill would go out when they left to see if they could find any money between the rocks.

The family was often isolated during icy periods in winter, and sometimes horse-drawn sleighs could be seen traveling over the ice to some of the nearby islands. If any family members were onshore and couldn't return because of the weather, they stayed at a friend's house. Ray started school during the last year the family lived at the lighthouse, but he had to repeat the first grade because he missed so many days when it was impossible to get to the school.

Evelyn Holbrook died in October 1917, and the family watched sadly as the casket was carried across the breakwater to the shore. One of Ray Holbrook's last memories of the lighthouse was November 11, 1918, when whistles blew from every boat and factory in the area at 11:00 a.m. to celebrate the end of World War I.

The light was electrified in 1934, and the job of tending the station went to the keeper at Spring Point Ledge. The last keeper at Portland Breakwater was Preston L. Marr, the son and grandson of keepers at Hendricks Head Light.

The keeper's house on the breakwater was demolished in late February 1935. In the early 1940s, shipyards expanded into the harbor, shortening the breakwater until the lighthouse stood only 100 feet from the shore.

Portland Breakwater Light was extinguished in 1942, like many lighthouses during World War II. The fog bell was operated electrically for a while, but the electrical cable was badly damaged by dredging operations. It was subsequently decided, in May 1943, that the light and fog signal were no longer needed for local navigation.

The lighthouse was declared surplus property and was sold into private hands. For some years, the Greater Portland Public Development Commission owned the lighthouse and adjacent land, and the General Electric Company leased the property and maintained a facility nearby.

In 1985, Al Glickman of Spring Point Associates donated the property to the City of South Portland. The Maine Historical Preservation Commission secured $26,000 from the Lighthouse Bicentennial Fund and the South Portland–Cape Elizabeth Rotary Club; the funds paid for a 1989 renovation of the lighthouse that included structural repairs and a new coat of paint. A park has been established adjacent to the lighthouse, officially named Bug Light Park.

A Liberty Ship memorial in the park, sponsored by the Portland Harbor Museum, was dedicated in November 2001. A total of 274 ships were built on the site during World War II. Most of them were Liberty Ships, which played an important role carrying supplies across the Atlantic during the war. Interpretive signs at the memorial tell the story of the ships built in South Portland.

Through the 1990s, the tower's condition deteriorated and the ventilator ball was stolen from the top of the lantern. The South Portland–Cape Elizabeth Rotary Club and the Spring Point Ledge Light Trust completed a new restoration that culminated in a relighting ceremony on August 14, 2002. A replacement ventilator ball was

installed, donated by the U.S. Coast Guard Aids to Navigation Team South Portland. The tower was painted inside and out, and a 250-millimeter optic was added. William Dale, the mayor of South Portland, declared at the relighting ceremony, "This harbor is alive and well, and this lighthouse is representative of it."

Jack Roberts, president of the South Portland–Cape Elizabeth Rotary Club and chairman of the town council of neighboring Cape Elizabeth, added, "Bug Light has a new lease on life. It will shine as the crown jewel of Bug Light Park. . . . This lighthouse

Many people toured the lighthouse on August 14, 2002, the day it was relighted. *Photo by the author.*

is so much more than stone and iron. It is living history. This lighthouse has stood the test of time for 127 years. With loving care it will be here for another century and beyond."

Senior Chief Tommy Dutton of U.S. Coast Guard Aids to Navigation Team South Portland had the honor of turning on the light at the event. The lighthouse now exhibits a white flash every four seconds, welcoming visitors to South Portland and historic Portland Harbor.

To reach Bug Light Park, follow Broadway in South Portland to its northern end. When you reach the stop sign in front of the Spring Point Marina, turn left. Turn right onto Madison Street and follow it into Bug Light Park. Bear right to the free parking along the water, near the lighthouse.

You can also see the unusual little lighthouse from many excursion boats leaving Portland Harbor. The Lighthouse Lovers Cruise offered by Portland Discovery passes close by; visit www.portlanddiscovery.com or call (207) 774-0808. The amphibious vehicle tours of Downeast Duck Adventures offer a view; call (207) 774- 3825 or visit www.downeastduck-tours.com. Lucky Catch Lobstering provides lighthouse photo opportunities while guiding you through the daily routines of Maine lobstermen; call (207) 233-2026 or visit www.luckycatch.com.

On the edge of Bug Light Park is the South Portland Historical Society's museum in the historic Cushing's Point House. The museum features exhibits on the history of the Liberty shipyards in South Portland, local lighthouses and their keepers, South Portland's role in the Civil War, and more. Admission is free, and there's a gift shop on the site. Open daily May through October and on weekends in November and December. Call (207) 767-7299 for more information.

CHAPTER 11

Halfway Rock Light in October 2007. *Photo by the author.*

Halfway Rock Light

1871

Halfway Rock is a windswept, uneven ledge far out in Casco Bay, in the middle of coastal shipping lanes, almost eight miles east of the entrance to Portland Harbor. The ledge stretches for about a quarter of a mile to the southwest and to the north from the lighthouse location, most of it lurking menacingly just under the surface. Its name comes from its location, about halfway between Cape Elizabeth, to the west-southwest, and Cape Small in Phippsburg, to the east-northeast.

The ledge claimed many vessels, including the brig *Samuel* in the spring of 1835. Agitation for an aid to navigation in the vicinity began as early as 1837, when Capt. Joseph Smith, in command of a U.S. revenue cutter, recommended the construction of a stone monument because of the dangers the ledge presented in hazy and foggy weather. It wasn't until March 1869 that Congress appropriated $50,000 for the construction of a lighthouse.

Temporary quarters for the crew were constructed at the ledge. Two major storms in September and October 1869 slowed construction, but the foundation for the tower was finished by the end of the year. Work resumed the following spring and the tower was nearly completed in August, when the project hit a financial snag.

The 1870 annual report of the Lighthouse Board announced, "The site is isolated, and consequently the landing of materials and the employment of laborers were more than ordinarily difficult and expensive." The work crew had to be dismissed when funds ran out, and all the equipment and materials were removed from the site and put into storage.

An additional $10,000 was appropriated in March 1871, and the 76-foot granite tower was completed that summer. The construction of the tower was similar to that of Massachusetts' Minot's Ledge Light, where massive granite blocks are dovetailed together. The granite was quarried at Chebeague Island, and the blocks were prepared at Fort Scammel in Portland Harbor.

The lighthouse originally held a third-order Fresnel lens, exhibiting a white light punctuated by a red flash every minute. The light went to service on August 15, 1871. The first keeper was Capt. John T. Sterling, a relative of Robert Thayer Sterling, author of the book

Lighthouses of the Maine Coast and the Men Who Keep Them. Years later, John Sterling's daughter recalled how she would anxiously walk to the shore of Peaks Island in Portland, where the family lived, to watch for her father's arrival after days or weeks at the light station.

Sterling's two assistant keepers were James Jones and Albert F. Purrington. The keepers lived in rooms inside the tower on the barren, two-acre island. Another one of the early assistants, Sylvanus E. Doyle, was dismissed in 1873 for vacating the station without permission, leaving Sterling alone. Sterling told the district inspector that Doyle had given him "a great deal of trouble."

George A. Toothaker, a native of nearby Harpwsell, Maine, described as "bronzed and fissured even as the gray and seaweed-stained granite of the Rock itself," was an assistant keeper beginning in 1872 and principal keeper from 1883 to 1885. "My first day was almost like my last," he told a newspaper reporter. "Me, it affected mentally. Others it affects physically, and I have known of one case where it has driven a man insane." Toothaker may have been referring to himself; the strain of life on the Rock obviously had a deep and profound effect on him.

In October 1885, the district lighthouse inspector wrote to the chairman of the Lighthouse Board to inform him that Toothaker had not spoken to William Tarlton Holbrook, an assistant keeper, for periods of a week or longer. Toothaker said he had nothing against Holbrook, but that there were times when he simply preferred not to speak. Holbrook told the inspector that Toothaker was "at times out

Early view of Halfway Rock Light Station. *From the collection of the author.*

of his mind, or on the verge of so being." On two occasions, Toothaker had suddenly left the station and rowed to his home at Harpswell, leaving Holbrook alone.

Holbrook expressed a fear that Toothaker might attack him, and the inspector agreed that Toothaker had "a natural tendency to insanity, which his lonely life on the Rock had aggravated." At the inspector's urging, Toothaker soon resigned, and Holbrook became the principal keeper. Toothaker didn't let go of his responsibilities easily; he wrote to the Lighthouse Board charging that Holbrook had allowed the light to go out. Interviewed years after he had left Halfway Rock, Toothaker said: "Asleep or awake, the beacon haunts you. Often I would start, quick, sharp, out of profound sleep, a great, dark haunting shudder on me—the light has gone out. Even now it is my fear, and so nervous am I of a night that all sounds startle me, even though it is years since I left the Rock."

A whistling buoy that was positioned near the light station certainly didn't help Toothaker's woes. Its doleful sound was compared in an 1885 article in the *Boston Globe* to the "sad efforts of a despairing mule." The writer declared that if he obtained a keeper's position at Halfway Rock, his first aim would be "to choke that whistle during the first week of my residence there or die in the vain attempt."

Holbrook was principal keeper until 1890. His troubles weren't over with Toothaker's resignation; one of his assistants once became so delirious with a fever that Holbrook had to lock him in a room in the lighthouse.

Mary Bradford Crowninshield's 1886 book, *All Among the Lighthouses,* described the visit of a lighthouse tender to Halfway Rock when Holbrook was in charge. When a boy on board expressed his desire to become a lighthouse keeper, the keeper responded, "Guess ye wouldn't keep in that frame of mind long, sonny, ef ye tried one week of it. . . . It's mighty tough and lonely sometimes, but my! We're on shore compared to them folks out to Mt. Desert Rock!"

Crowninshield went on to describe the lighthouse interior:

> *The first room entered was the kitchen of the establishment. There, every thing looked in the best possible order, with its neat pantry, finely polished cooking stove, and shining utensils. The next flight of stairs brought them to another room, the bedroom of the principal keeper; and above this was a second room, with two beds for the assistant keepers. A fourth flight of stairs brought them out into the watch-room, where the keeper on duty remains all night, to see that the light does not go out, and to keep guard generally. In this room*

there was a stove, a chair, a table, and a small lamp. It contained also the driving clock, commonly called the "flash clock," whose mechanism operated the flash light. for such is the "characteristic," as it is called, of the light at Half-way Rock.

The station got its first fog signal when a 43-foot, pyramidal, skeleton-type bell tower was bolted to the rock near the lighthouse in 1887, with a 1,000-pound fog bell and striking machinery. A raised walkway connected the bell tower to the lighthouse. Soon after its construction, the bell tower survived a fierce December storm that buried Halfway Rock under eight feet of water. During that same month, the schooner *John James,* bound for Steuben, Maine, broke apart and sank near Halfway Rock. The captain and crew escaped safely and rowed 14 miles to shore.

In 1888, a new boathouse, with an 18-by-24-foot foundation, was built. Its upper story contained two additional rooms of living space for the keepers. This improved the living conditions, but the tower was always the safest place in a storm. Two years later, an oil house, 8 feet square, was built and secured 20 feet above the rock on a skeletal wooden frame, securely bolted to the ledge.

The fog bell proved inadequate in rough weather, so it was replaced in 1905 by a powerful Daboll trumpet operated by diesel engines. It was reported in 1907 that the signal was in operation for 796 hours during the previous year and consumed 504 gallons of oil.

Reaching the mainland for supplies required an 11-mile row to Portland, often made difficult or impossible by rough seas or ice. In February 1934, the keepers reported that ice an inch thick extended all the way past Halfway Rock. Eventually, under the Coast Guard, a buoy tender out of South Portland delivered supplies each week.

Arthur Strout, of the famous lightkeeping Strout family mainly identified with Portland Head Light, was an assistant keeper from 1929 to 1934. He was promoted to principal keeper and was the last civilian in

Early-1900s postcard view of Halfway Rock Light. *From the collection of the author.*

Coast Guardsman Ken Rouleau at Halfway Rock, 1960. *Courtesy of Ken Rouleau.*

that position. When the Coast Guard took over management of the station in 1939, Strout joined that branch of the service and remained in charge until 1945. The light was not in operation for three years during World War II; the blackout ended on June 28, 1945.

Around 1936, Strout struck up a friendship over the radio with 19-year-old Pereley A. Swasey Jr., an amateur radio operator in Falmouth, Maine. Strout was ashore during a May 1936 storm, and he feared for the welfare of the assistant keeper on duty as well as the buildings and equipment at the station. Telephone communication was down, so Strout went to Swasey's home. With the young man's help he was able to contact the assistant keeper, John Pendell, after two hours of trying. Pendell was fine, but the boat slip was damaged. Strout got word to the authorities and repairs were soon completed.

Ken Rouleau of Derry, New Hampshire, was barely out of his teens when he arrived at the station in 1960 as a Coast Guard keeper. At that time the small living quarters were inside the upper story of the boathouse and simply consisted of a bedroom and a kitchen. For a young Coast Guardsman, the isolated station wasn't ideal duty. "We didn't have any fun—I didn't, anyway," he said in a 2002 interview. "There was not much social life. You took care of yourself."

The days were split into 12-hour shifts for the two men on the station, so the crew members didn't see that much of each other. But some of the men made an impression on Rouleau. He remembered James Murray from Manchester, New Hampshire. And he definitely remembered John Cluff, a native of the southern Maine coast. This may have something to do with the fact that Cluff was a great cook—he made "the most delicious sausage you've ever tasted." His other specialties included asparagus on toast and peach pies.

The Coast Guard sent a large boat to pick the men up or take them to the station, but it was necessary to transfer to a small peapod boat to land at Halfway Rock. It took great skill to land the boat on the ramp in heavy seas. Rouleau recalled one time when Cluff was returning with the station's television, which had just been repaired on the mainland. The boat flipped over as he tried to land, and Rouleau got a sinking feeling as he watched and thought, "No TV for another three weeks!" Launching the peapod was just as hazardous, as the men would ride it down the steep ramp. "It flipped more than once," said Rouleau.

The Coast Guard crew kept the third-order Fresnel lens and all the brass in the tower spotlessly clean. Every 30 minutes, they checked the clocks associated with the mechanisms that turned the lens. There were three clockwork mechanisms that had to be wound once a day. The fog signal also had to be operated as needed. "The foghorn would drive you completely bonkers when it would be foggy for seven or eight days at a time," said Rouleau.

Storms frequently did great damage at the exposed location. One gale in December 1945 bent two 60-foot steel radio towers to the ground. On February 18, 1972, a severe winter storm washed away a fuel tank for the generator, leaving the crew without power or heat for some time. A walkway and part of the boat ramp were also destroyed, and the crew had to be taken off by helicopter.

During a spell of murky weather in July 1972, the *Kennebec Journal* reported that Coast Guard keepers hadn't been able to see any land from the station for an extended period. "We saw a small section of Jewell Island for a few minutes one day," said Frank Reese of Bath, Maine, "but that's been it for land." The station's foghorn had been blasting for 10 seconds every minute for about two weeks. "You just learn to live with it, and think about something else," said Reese.

One of the last keepers was Stephen Krikorian, also a Maine native. In 1975, the 27-year-old Krikorian told the *Portland Press Herald* about some of the unusual ways the keepers passed the lonely hours. He picked up a basketball that had washed ashore. "There are 2,448 pimples on this," he said. "I counted 'em. It took a day." The men kept a chart in the house with the heading "House Fly Killings." One of the other crewmen, Ronald Handfield, held the record of 257 fly killings in two months.

One day, the men tried to cure their boredom by cleaning up all the wood on the island, which they burned and dumped into the water. The next day, the charred remains of the wood came floating back onto the ledge with high tide.

At the time of the 1975 article, the Coast Guard crewmen spent two weeks on the station followed by a week off. The men maintained the equipment and buildings and radioed in weather reports to South Portland every three hours. They tried to bring enough clothes for the two-week stay, but Krikorian once tried washing his pants by tying them to the boat slip and letting the tides do the job. "I lost every one of them," he said.

The keepers were removed for good later in 1975, and the light was automated with a modern DCB-224 optic. The third-order Fresnel lens was carried to Connecticut in the hold of the Coast Guard cutter *Eagle,* and it was put on display at the museum at the Coast Guard Academy in New London.

The lighthouse tower now stands alone on Halfway Rock, still an active aid to navigation. Storms have destroyed the other structures. Most recently, the station's marine railway was destroyed by the "perfect storm" of October 1991.

In the late 1990s, under the Maine Lights Program, the station was to be turned over to a local nonprofit group or community, but there were no applicants. In May 2000, the American Lighthouse Foundation was licensed by the Coast Guard to care for the tower.

An April 2007 storm damaged the attached wooden building. In June 2004, Maine Preservation included this lighthouse on its list of the state's most endangered properties. At this writing in early 2013, the lighthouse is slated to be transferred to a new owner under the guidelines of the National Historic Lighthouse Preservation Act. If no nonprofit organizations or communities apply for ownership, the property will be offered to the general public via an online auction.

This dramatic lighthouse can be seen very distantly from the Portland Observatory and from some of the tour boats leaving Portland. For a closer look, you can charter a cruise with Sea Escape Cottages and Charters of Bailey Island; call (207) 833-5531 or visit www.seaescapecottages.com.

CHAPTER 12

The WLV-612 was built at the Curtis Bay Coast Guard Yard, Baltimore, Maryland, in the summer of 1950 *(top photo, U.S. Coast Guard)*. It served as the Portland Lightship from 1971 to 1975. It later served on the Nantucket Shoals, Massachusetts, and is now a privately owned charter vessel. *Bottom photo (2006) by the author.*

Miscellaneous Lights and Lightships

Seavey's Island Range Lights, 1894–1905

After several petitions, the Lighthouse Board made an argument for a light station at Henderson Point, at the extreme southwest point of Seavey's Island on the Piscataqua River in Kittery, on the north side of the channel to Portsmouth, New Hampshire. "It is often very difficult to locate Henderson Point at night and in thick weather; the channel is narrow and there is a strong tide at this point, where the course changes. The commercial statistics for Portsmouth Harbor indicate about 5,000 vessels arriving and departing annually, transporting about 610,000 tons of freight."

After a congressional appropriation of $3,800, a range light station was established at Henderson Point in 1894. The fixed white lights, exhibited from simple posts, served to guide vessels between Seavey's Island and Goat Island Ledge. The rear tower, a red post, carried two lights, one above the other, with focal planes of 23 and 31 feet. The front tower was a white post with a single light 15 feet above mean high water.

There was a resident keeper at the station; the keeper in 1897 was John W. Wetzel, who went on to serve 27 years as an assistant keeper at Whaleback Light. The station was discontinued when Henderson Point was destroyed in 1905 to widen the channel.

After a brief time as keeper of the Seavey's Island Range Lights, John Wetzel was an assistant keeper at Whaleback Light for 27 years. *Courtesy of the Maine Lighthouse Museum.*

Kennebunk Pier Light, 1857

A navigational light was established on January 1, 1857, at the mouth of the Kennebunk River, on Kennebunk Pier. The lighthouse, which held a sixth-order Fresnel lens 25 feet above sea level, was described as a "square wooden structure, painted white, having a lantern on the outer end." The characteristic was fixed red, to keep the light from being confused with the fixed white light at Goat Island, about two miles to the northeast.

There was never a resident keeper; local men were employed as caretakers or "lamplighters." The original structure was destroyed many years ago, but an automated light on a skeleton tower remains in service at the river's mouth.

Portland Lightship, 1903–1975

Prompted by a boom in shipping entering Portland Harbor in the late 1800s (nearly 5,000 vessels in 1897), Congress saw fit to appropriate $90,000 for a lightship off Cape Elizabeth. The station was established in March 1903, about five miles southeast of the twin light station at Cape Elizabeth. It was known as the Cape Elizabeth Lightship until 1912, when the name was changed to the Portland Lightship.

The first vessel on the site was the LV-74, a 129-foot-long, two-masted, wooden-hulled ship. The LV-74 remained on the station until 1931, and it survived several calamities. It parted anchor and drifted several times, and it suffered minor damage in fires in 1911 and 1920, both times while undergoing repairs. After it was replaced by the LV-90 in 1931, the LV-74 was employed as a relief vessel until it was retired in 1933.

The 135-foot-long LV-90, a two-masted, steel-hulled vessel, served on the station until 1942. The LV-90 served as an examination vessel during World War II, and after the war it was eventually returned to the Portland station. A buoy had marked the site during most of the war years. The LV-90 was retired in 1952.

Three more lightships served on the Portland station: the LV-111 (1952–69), the LV-114 (1969–71), and the WLV-612 (1971–75). Only the WLV-612 still exists. After the Portland station was discontinued, the 128-foot-long, two-masted, steel-hulled vessel served until 1983 on the Nantucket Shoals, Massachusetts. It was the last lightship in use in the United States.

The WLV-612 has passed through a number of owners in subsequent years. Its present owner, William Golden, is a lawyer and former Massachusetts state senator. The vessel is now available for private charters or events; see www.nantucketlightship.com or call (617) 821-6771 for details.

Little Mark Island Monument, 1827

The Little Mark Island Monument in October 2007. *Photo by the author.*

In 1827, a pyramidal granite day-beacon, about 50 feet tall, was erected on Little Mark Island in Casco Bay, not far from Bailey's Island. A room in the lower portion of the beacon became known as the Mariners' Refuge; it was apparently intended to serve as a shelter for shipwrecked sailors.

At some point in its history, a navigational light was added to the top of the beacon. An automated light is still in use today, with a white flash every four seconds. Coast Guard crews access the light by climbing a ladder on the side of the tower.

SELECTED BIBLIOGRAPHY

For more detailed bibliographies for each lighthouse, visit www.newenglandlighthouses.net.

Books

Adamson, Hans Christian. *Keepers of the Lights*. New York: Greenberg, 1955.

Bachelder, Peter Dow. *Lighthouses of Casco Bay*. Portland, ME: Breakwater Press, 1975.

Caldwell, Bill. *Lighthouses of Maine*. Portland, ME: Gannett Books, 1986.

Cape Elizabeth Historical Preservation Society. *Cape Elizabeth Past to Present*. Cape Elizabeth, ME: Town of Cape Elizabeth, 1991.

Clifford, J. Candace, and Mary Louise Clifford. *Maine Lighthouses: Documentation of Their Past*. Alexandria, VA: Cypress Communications 2005.

Clifford, Mary Louise and J. Candace Clifford. *Women Who Kept the Lights: An Illustrated History of Female Lighthouse Keepers*. Williamsburg, VA: Cypress Communications, 1993.

Crowninshield, Mary Bradford. *All Among the Lighthouses*. Boston: D. Lothrop Company, 1886.

De Wire, Elinor. *Guardians of the Lights: The Men and Women of the U.S. Lighthouse Service*, Sarasota, FL: Pineapple Press, 1995.

Drake, Samuel Adams. *The Pine Tree Coast*. Boston: Estes and Lauriat, 1891.

Elwell, Edward H. *Elwell's Portland and Vicinity*. Portland, ME: Greater Portland Landmarks, Inc., 1975.

Feller-Roth, Barbara. *Lighthouses: A Guide to Many of Maine's Coastal and Offshore Guardians*. Freeport, ME: DeLorme Mapping Company, 1988.

Finnegan, Kathleen E. and Timothy E. Harrison. *Lighthouses of Maine and New Hampshire*. Laconia, New Hampshire: Quantum Printing Corporation, 1991.

Holland, Francis Ross, Jr. *America's Lighthouses: An Illustrated History*. New York: Dover Publications, Inc., 1972.

Holland, F. Ross. *Great American Lighthouses*. Washington, D.C.: The Preservation Press, 1989.

Jordan, William B. *A History of Cape Elizabeth, Maine*. Bowie, MD: Heritage Books, Inc., 1987 (facsimile reprint edition). Originally published 1965.

Labrie, Rose Cushing. *Sentinel of the Sea: Nubble Light*. Hampton, NH: Hampton Publishing Company, 1958.

Marcus, Jon. *Lighthouses of New England*. Stillwater, MN: Voyageur Press, 2001.

Noble, Dennis L. *Lighthouses & Keepers*. Annapolis: Naval Institute Press, 1997.

Porter, Jane Molloy. *Friendly Edifices: Piscataqua Lighthouses and Other Aids to Navigation*. Portsmouth, NH: Peter E. Randall Publisher, 2006.

Putnam, George R. *Lighthouses and Lightships of the United States*. Boston: Houghton Mifflin, 1933.

Rich, Louise Dickinson. *The Coast of Maine*. New York: Thomas Y. Crowell Company, 1956.

Rummler, Kathleen G. *Portland Head Light: Maine's Oldest Lighthouse*. Cape Elizabeth, Maine: The Museum at Portland Head Light, 1997.

Shattuck, Clifford. *The Nubble: Cape Neddick Lightstation, York, Maine*. Freeport, ME: The Cumberland Press, Inc., 1979.

Simpson, Dorothy. *The Maine Islands in Story and Legend*. Nobleboro, ME: Blackberry Books, 1987.

Small, Connie. *The Lighthouse Keeper's Wife*. Orono, Maine: The University of Maine Press, 1986.

Snow, Edward Rowe. *Famous Lighthouses of America*. New York: Dodd, Mead & Company, 1955.

Snow, Edward Rowe. *Famous Lighthouses of New England*. 1945. Updated edition (as *The Lighthouses of New England*), Beverly, MA: Commonwealth Editions, 2002.

Snow, Edward Rowe. *Mysteries and Adventures Along the Atlantic Coast*. New York: Dodd, Mead & Company, 1948. Updated edition, Beverly, MA: Commonwealth Editions, 2006.

Snow, Edward Rowe. *The Romance of Casco Bay*. New York: Dodd, Mead & Company, 1975.

Snow, Edward Rowe. *Strange Tales from Nova Scotia to Cape Hatteras*. New York: Dodd, Mead & Company, 1949.

Snow, Edward Rowe. *Women of the Sea*. New York: Dodd, Mead and Company, 1962.

Sterling, Robert Thayer. *Lighthouses of the Maine Coast and the Men Who Keep Them*. Brattleboro, VT: Stephen Daye Press, 1935.

Thompson, Kenneth E., Jr. *Portland Head Light and Fort Williams*. Portland, Maine: The Thompson Group, 1998.

Thomson, William O. *Nubble Light: Cape Neddick Light Station*. Kennebunk, ME: 'Scapes Me, 2000.

Thomson, William O. *Solitary Vigils at Boon Island*. Kennebunk, ME: 'Scapes Me, 2000.

Willoughby, Malcolm F. *Lighthouses of New England*. Boston: T.O. Metcalf Company, 1929.

Winslow, Sidney L. *Fish Scales and Stone Chips*. Portland, ME: Machigonne Press, 1952.

Wood, Pamela. *The Salt Book*. New York: Anchor Books, 1977.

Wright, Sarah Bird. *Islands of the Northeastern United States and Canada*. Atlanta, Georgia: Peachtree Publishers, LTD., 1990.

Newspapers, magazines, and other periodicals

Annual reports of the Light-House Board, 1852-1906.
Bangor Daily News, various articles 1967-2006.
Bangor Whig and Courier, various articles 1866-82.
Down East, various articles 1959-91.
Eastern Argus, various articles 1830-36.
Island Journal, annual publication of the Island Institute, 1987-2006.
The Keeper's Log, various articles 1984-2008.
Kennebec Journal, various articles 1886-1972.
Lighthouse Digest, various articles 1994-2008.
Lighthouse Service Bulletin, 1929-35.
Maine Coast Fisherman, various articles 1948-51.
New England Magazine, various articles 1886-95.
New Hampshire Gazette, various articles 1829-49.
New York Times, various articles 1889-1988.
Portland Press Herald, various articles 1947-2000.
Portsmouth Herald, various articles 1890-1999.
Portsmouth Journal, various articles 1827-1911.
Shore Village Museum Newsletter, 1988-97.
Soundings, various articles 1984-2008.
Washington Post, various articles 1897-1936.
Yankee, various articles 1956-2003.
York County Coast Star, various articles 1997.

Web sites
American Lighthouse Foundation, www.lighthousefoundation.org
The Lighthouse Directory, www.unc.edu/~rowlett/lighthouse/
Lighthouse Friends, www.Lighthousefriends.com
New England Lighthouses: A Virtual Guide, www.newenglandlighthouses.net

INDEX

Page numbers given in *italics* indicate illustrations.

CPSIA information can be obtained at www.ICGtesting.com
Printed in the USA
BVOW02s2202230315

392993BV00009B/27/P